PROFILES *OF* VALOR

2

Character Studies
from the
War of Independence

I0869431

Marilyn Boyer &
Grace Tumas Ehrman

Master Books First Printing: November 2025

Copyright © 2025 by Marilyn Boyer and Grace Tumas Ehrman. All rights reserved. No part of this book may be reproduced, copied, broadcast, stored, or shared in any form whatsoever without written permission from the publisher, except in the case of brief quotations in articles and reviews. For information write:

Master Books, P.O. Box 726, Green Forest, AR 72638

Master Books® is a division of the
New Leaf Publishing Group, LLC.

ISBN: 978-1-68344-426-8
ISBN: 978-1-61458-945-7 (digital)

All scripture verses are from the King James Version of the Bible.

Please consider requesting that a copy of this volume be purchased by your local library system.

Printed in the United States of America

Please visit our website for other great titles:
www.masterbooks.com

For information regarding promotional opportunities, please contact the publicity department at pr@nlpg.com.

PROFILES OF VALOR

Character Studies
from the
War of Independence

December 1775 - December 1777

Credits

Thanks to the following people for their investment in helping to preserve these inspiring stories from America's past. It is my prayer that their efforts will reap a bountiful harvest as these stories will serve to be an inspiration to those in whose hands America's future lies!

I wish to thank David Barton, who has been such an inspiration to me, personally, to become excited about learning about our godly heritage. God has gifted him for such a time as this in our country. He is the master of primary source documents! Tuesday night has traditionally been "Barton night" in our home as we gather to watch his DVDs and invite friends in to learn with us! It is only as we get truth back into the public square that we can hope to preserve the heritage of freedom handed down to us.

Thanks to Grace Tumas Ehrman, for her role in crafting these stories in such a way that they are a delight to read! It's great when even the editors have to read the stories first to see what happens and then go back and edit!

Thanks to my dear friend Mary Ann Edman who is the world's most efficient multi-tasker, committed to producing quality that will be a tribute to our

Lord and Savior. Her creativity has been indispensable in producing the layout and graphic design for this book as well as editing the mistakes the rest of us overlooked!

Thanks to Judy Saunders, my long-time friend and prayer warrior, for her faithful work in the tedious editing process. God has gifted her with a precise eye for detail. She sees things I just don't notice. Thanks, my friend!

Thanks to my son, Rick, who, despite his incredibly busy life, has read these stories to his children at night, while editing each for accuracy of content to assure we are portraying these men and women in an worthy manner, giving honor where honor is due.

Chronological Table of Contents

Table of Contents by Character Quality

Introduction

Why did the Founding Fathers feel compelled to risk their lives to enter the conflict known as the War of Independence? Was it purely because of taxation without representation as we would be led to believe today? Absolutely not. That's the 17th reason in a list of 29 usurpations listed in the Declaration of Independence. Something very sacred and dear—their liberty—was at stake, not their pocketbook. They believed they had a duty to protect it.

Separation from Great Britain was not decided upon hastily. The colonists had been militarily attacked for more than two years before they finally announced a separation; and for eleven years preceding that announcement (from 1765 to 1776), they had diligently pursued reconciliation. Another appeal was sent in 1775. The Olive Branch Petition, a detailed appeal was sent in May 1776. Their appeals were submitted in a respectful manner, desiring for reconciliation to be made and affirming their allegiance to King George III.

The Rev. Peter Powers, in a sermon he preached in front of the Vermont Legislature in 1778, specifically noted that America had "taken up arms in its own defense"—that she had not initiated the conflict but was only defending herself after being attacked.[1]

The Continental Congress also issued a manifesto reflecting a similar tone of submission to God:

> *We, therefore, the Congress of the United States of America, do solemnly declare and proclaim that . . . [we] appeal to the God Who searcheth the hearts of men for the rectitude of our intentions; and in His holy presence declare that, as we are not moved by any light or hasty suggestions of anger or revenge, so through every possible change of fortune we will adhere to this our determination.*[2]

The Rev. Dr. John Witherspoon (also a signer of the Declaration) likewise affirmed:

> *On the part of America, there was not the most distant thought of subverting the government or of hurting the interest of the people of Great Britain, but of defending their own privileges from unjust encroachment; there was not the least desire of withdrawing their allegiance from the common sovereign [King George III] till it became absolutely necessary—and indeed, it was his own choice.*[3]

Consider, as Dr. Witherspoon correctly noted:

> *. . . [I]t was Great Britain who broke the entreaties. America's peaceful appeals were responded to with armed military force. King George III dispatched 25,000 British troops to invade his own Colonies,*

enter the homes of his own citizens to take their private possessions and goods, and imprison them without trials—all in violation of his own British Common Law, English Bill of Rights, and Magna Carta [centuries old documents that formed the basis of the covenant between British rulers and citizens]. Only when those governmental covenants had been broken by their rulers and America had been directly attacked did the Americans respond in self-defense.[4]

This book is full of true stories of people who answered the call to defend freedom, and many paid an incredible price to obtain the liberties we enjoy today, but it is more than that. These patriots serve as examples to us of courage, boldness, and valor, and many more character qualities that we would do well to try to incorporate into our lives. As you read their profiles it is my hope that you will be inspired to make the sacrifices necessary to see that these patriots did not sacrifice in vain.

Marilyn Boyer

Perseverance

DEFINITION

Steadfastness despite unexpected obstacles

MEMORY VERSE

Therefore, my beloved brethren,
be ye stedfast, unmoveable, always
abounding in the work of the Lord,
forasmuch as ye know that your labour
is not in vain in the Lord.

I Corinthians 15:58

The Noble Train

Gen. Henry Knox

Fort Ticonderoga & Boston,
Massachusetts
December, 1775

The young artillery officer trudged through the snow towards the headquarters of the Continental Army. Several miles away, the city of Boston, guarded by Lord William Howe's British Navy, crouched immobile, locked in ice. General Washington, holding the city under siege, had no large guns to occupy Dorchester Heights above Boston and shell the British. Twenty-five-year-old Colonel Henry Knox, who had previously worked as a Boston bookseller and an artillery expert, had hatched a daring plan to force the Redcoats out of Massachusetts' "city on a hill." Facing his Commander-in-Chief, Knox announced that he knew where to locate enough guns to try to take Boston. Seven months ago, in May 1775, Ethan Allen's Green Mountain Boys surprised the British at Fort Ticonderoga on Lake Champlain and forced them to surrender. Since then, the fifty-nine pieces of artillery captured with the fort had lain unused three hundred miles to the north. Knox suggested that he organize an operation to travel to Ticonderoga, load up the cannons and carry them back to score a much-needed victory against the British.

Washington's advisors shook their heads. The plan would never work, they argued. Knox would have to dismount the guns, drag them onto barges, and then ferry them down Lake George before the great, thirty-mile-long lake froze over. Even if Knox managed to do that, he would still be faced with the daunting task of hauling the cannons by oxen and sledge over three hundred miles of rough, possibly snowless trails. It would be almost impossible to have an unbelievable combination of the right weather that would both keep the lake from freezing and provide snow for the sleds. Despite his advisors' misgivings, Washington agreed to Knox's plan. The operation would take a large military corps to assemble a flotilla of flat-bottomed gundalows to transport the cannons by water. In addition to this, Knox needed forty large sleds, each weighing 5,400 pounds, and eighty teams of oxen to pull them. If Knox could pull the operation off, it would give the American army a tremendous advantage over the British, stubbornly holed up in Boston, and protected by their navy in Boston Harbor.

Colonel Henry Knox

Knox immediately set off on horseback, accompanied by his nineteen-year-old brother William and a servant named Miller, and arrived at Fort Ticonderoga on the evening of December 5, 1775. At dawn on December 6, Knox began to move the guns, assisted by the garrison at Ticonderoga. As they began looking over the cannons, Knox and his men found that the ancient carriages, dating from the French and Indian War, were weak and rotten from exposure to the weather during the past year. Knox ordered the guns dismounted from their rotten carriages and moved from the fort for reassembly at the *Place d'Arms.* When they finished, they had forty-three heavy brass and iron guns, eight mortars, two howitzers, and six cohorns, or portable mortars.

24-pounder bronze siege cannon

Knox moved the heaviest cannons first, hauling them by oxcart to a gundalow tied up at the

Flat-bottomed gundalow used to transport cannons

King's dock just below the fort. After he finished loading them, Knox sent the gundalow around the Fort Ticonderoga peninsula and into the LaChute River. From there, the crew would navigate down the Portage Road from Lake Champlain to Fort George and drop off their load, then sail back for more cannons. Knox supervised the guns' overland route while the gundalow ferried steadily back and forth to the mouth of Lake George, carrying the smaller cohorns first and then the mortars. At the Lake George Landing, a small flotilla organized to guide the cannons, transported on a flat-bottomed, barge-like scow, down the lake around 3 p.m. Meanwhile, the other bateau boats pushed on the

The ox train starts out from Fort George

next day, the men rowing hard for about four hours in a raging wind. Knox, ordering his servant to seize his baggage, clambered into a boat. They headed into a "fair wind," Knox noted. But the scow, sailing along behind, faced into a dying wind and ran aground. After four treacherous hours, the crew reached Sabbath Day Point at 9 p.m. on the evening of December 10th. The men scrambled ashore, blowing on their frozen hands, stamping their feet, and huddling around a warm fire in a hut. Although the Native Americans had gone to bed, they rose and roasted some venison over the coals for their guests. The men stretched out on the hut floor and spent the night with their backs to the fire.

They had failed to reach the southern end of the lake. If they did not cross the lake soon, the boats could not make the passage before the surface froze over like a sheet of glass. That night, Knox discovered that his scow had run aground on a submerged rock, but could be rescued if they had new strong ropes to pull her off the rocks. Since all their ropes had broken during the rescue operation, they had to send up to the fort for more ropes so that they could try to rescue the scow again in the morning. Half an hour after dawn, they rose again, and going out into the bitter wind, succeeded, after pushing hard for six long hours into the wind, in reaching the southern end of Lake George. Knox had hoped for the miracle of the comparatively mild weather to continue so that they could cross the lake. Now he needed the snow to come so that they could make the overland passage by sled. The ice must freeze solid by the time they reached the Hudson River, thick enough to support the 1800-pound weight of his biggest gun, the twenty-four pounder.

At Fort George, Knox began planning the movement of his guns by land. Sending a message to a neighboring squire, Knox asked for a number of sleds and oxen in order to drag the cannon when the first snow fell. He wanted to leave as soon as the first sleds appeared and the first white flakes began spiraling from the darkening winter sky. Confident that the sleds would arrive on time, Knox hurried back to the lake. Three days had passed since the scow encountered trouble on the rocks, and yet none of the vessels had arrived from Ticonderoga by December 13th. He had received no message. Unease prickled his spine. Anxiously, Knox sent out an express boat early that afternoon, only to learn that the scow had gotten off the treacherous rocks and struggled on to the Point, only to be sunk by a high wind and a raging sea on the night of the 10th. Despite this setback, all the rest of the guns arrived safely at Fort George between December 15 and 16, ten days after he first arrived at Ticonderoga. The lake had already begun to freeze. But no snow fell.

For the next two days of enforced waiting, Knox busied himself with transporting the guns into Fort George and firing off dispatches to Washington, detailing his progress. Staring out at the frozen lake, Knox admitted that he still did not know the best route to take the expedition out of New York. The sleds, however, would arrive on Tuesday or Wednesday. With these, Knox believed that they could glide along the frozen ground as far as Saratoga. After that, they would be forced to sit and wait for snow. Meanwhile, he had to send to Albany to obtain the rope with which to tether the cannons to the sleds.

Writing to Washington, Knox confidently stated: "We shall have a fine fall of snow . . . If that should be the case I hope . . . to be able to present your Excellency a noble train of artillery."

The noble train moves toward Boston

For the next six days, Knox apparently did not find the time to write in his diary. Instead, he must have awaited the arrival of the sleds, searched for teams, and waited for the anticipated snow that could smooth the roads and provide an overland passage. At some point, the colonel set off on foot for Fort Miller in order to check up on the arrival of the sleds and to negotiate with General Philip Schuyler about transporting the sleds through Albany. He then crossed the river by ferry to the west side, arriving at Saratoga in time for dinner. Crossing the ferry, the colonel felt the first snowflakes sting his face. Looking out during dinner, Knox saw to his joy that it was still snowing hard and fast. As they set off miles beyond Saratoga, the deepening snow on the roads almost prevented the horses from getting through.

Christmas Day dawned. Knox woke to find two feet of new white snow blanketing the ground. He was alone on Christmas Day. Realizing that the snowfall would make the journey by sled possible, Knox sent for a sleigh to continue south along unbroken roads. They had only gone two miles when the horses began to slow down, exhausted by plowing through the deep snow. Resignedly, Knox climbed out of the sleigh and trudged into the woods. He struggled along through the silver wilderness for four miles until he reached Squire Fisher's estate. Shivering and worn-out, he sat down to breakfast. Then he borrowed a horse, and rode in the bitter cold until he obtained a sleigh to take him to Albany. At Albany, Knox hurried to meet Schuyler. Between December 27–29, Knox and Schuyler hunted for two more teams and cannons to send north over the snow-covered roads. Schuyler, making use of his authority, sent men out into the countryside with

Colonel Knox brings the artillery into camp

orders to collect every sledge and horse they could find. These sleds and teams began arriving at Fort George and continued coming until January 1, 1776.

Unfortunately, the snow that allowed them to travel as far as Lansing's Ferry did not last, making it impossible to travel further south. Nevertheless, Knox had forty-two strong wooden sleds and eighty yoke of oxen set out down the road from Fort George. Desperate to keep the "noble train" moving in order to reach Washington in time, Knox even ordered his men to pour buckets of water from the river over the surface of the roads to freeze. Finally, on January 4th, the first guns, a brass twenty-four pounder and a small mortar, crossed the river at Lansing's Ferry and rolled into Albany. In spite of the thaw, they had transported four more cannons by the next day, and Knox hoped that the lingering ice would allow them to get as far as Springfield.

That afternoon, one of the heaviest cannons broke through the thin ice and plunged into the river at Half Moon Ferry. Alarmed, Knox sent the rest of the sleds around to a safer crossing at Sloss's Ferry on the Hudson. On January 7th, a second cannon crashed through the ice, but the men recovered it the next day. Moving cautiously now, barely breathing as the ice creaked beneath the sleds, the men, assisted by local townspeople, managed to get twenty sleds across in one day. On the morning of January 9th, with the train of sledges moving east, Knox rode on ahead. He had ceased to write much in his diary, making his daily movements difficult to ascertain.

Two days after leaving Claverack, Knox's train entered the Berkshires. The steep mountains, bare and brown without a covering of snow, discouraged the men in the front teams so that they refused to go further. Ahead, the precipice plunged sharply towards the Connecticut River valley. Undaunted,

Knox hired a new team of oxen, coaxing the grumbling crew to push on. As they kept pressing east, the news of their coming ran ahead of them like wildfire. As they passed through small colonial towns, the people ran out into the streets to watch them pass. In order to please a cheering crowd at Westfield, Knox loaded one of his large cannons with powder and fired it off. Knox and his "noble train" moved through on the Post Road, passing through the village of Claverack, and then proceeding east into Massachusetts.

Battling cold and exhaustion, Knox's artillery train glided from Great Barrington through the Massachusetts towns of Springfield, Wilbraham, Palmer, and Warren. Then they turned onto a route passing through the endless little towns of Brookfield, Spencer, Leicester, and Worcester. Diving back onto their original route, Knox's sledges trudged their way through Shrewsbury, Northborough, Marlborough, and Southborough before passing Framingham, Wayland, Weston, Waltham, and Watertown. The weather improved as they marched through Massachusetts, and the road became more passable. Finally, on January 24th, the tired but triumphant Continentals entered Cambridge.

When they arrived at Springfield, Knox hired new teamsters from Massachusetts since his New York crew needed to go home. Jubilantly, John

Adams watched as the noble artillery train rumbled through Framingham on January 25th. At last, on January 27, Colonel Knox entered Cambridge and went straight to Washington's headquarters with the news that the train had arrived! Knox had spent £521 on a journey he had believed would take two weeks and had instead spread out over ten rigorous weeks. In less than two months, Knox and his men maneuvered sixty tons of artillery across three hundred miles of rivers and lakes, over the Berkshire Mountains, and through ice and snow to plant on Dorchester Heights above Boston.

On the second week of March 1776, Washington had sufficient strength to bombard Boston from Dorchester Heights above the city, using the guns that Knox had painstakingly dragged all the way from Lake Champlain. The bombardment damaged the British sufficiently to force them to evacuate Boston and the American shores, and sail for Halifax, Nova Scotia. On March 18th, Washington's tattered Continental Army marched victoriously into the city. Knox, the enterprising young bookseller-turned-colonel, later became the Chief Artillery Officer in the Continental Army and later the first United States Secretary of War.

Henry Knox demonstrated incredible perseverance by devising and carrying out a heroic expedition which culminated in the evacuation of British forces from Boston and boosted morale during a low period of the American Revolution.

Questions

1. What plan did Knox present to Washington to supply him with cannons?
2. Why did Washington's advisors doubt it would work?
3. How many sleds and teams of oxen would be necessary to make the plan succeed?
4. How many guns were they able to salvage upon arriving at the fort?
5. Did the scow running aground discourage Knox? How did he rescue it?
6. How could they hope to carry the guns across the Hudson?
7. How did Knox demonstrate perseverance even after encountering difficulty, as reflected in the words he wrote to General Washington?
8. When did the snow begin to fall?
9. What plan did Knox determine to make work when the snow became too deep for his horses?
10. What did Knox order his men to do to keep moving when the snow stopped?
11. How did they get over the Berkshires?

Questions

12. How long did it take for Knox to complete his mission?
13. What was Washington able to accomplish upon receiving the cannons?
14. Tell of some of the obstacles Knox and his men faced and met with perseverance.
15. Think of a person in Scripture or history who demonstrated perseverance.

Perseverance accomplished what at first seemed impossible.

—Colonel Henry Knox

Valor

DEFINITION

Strength of spirit that enables
one to encounter danger with
firmness and gallantry

MEMORY VERSE

Have not I commanded thee?
Be strong and of a good courage;
be not afraid, neither be thou dismayed:
for the LORD thy God is with thee
whithersoever thou goest.

Joshua 1:9

Night of Fog

Gen. George Washington

Boston, Massachusetts
March 2–5, 1776

Winter winds brought snow and an anxious longing for home. Every day, another Continental Army soldier slipped away from the others, his footprints leading out of camp a silent testimony to the hardships of wartime America. At his headquarters' camp, outside of Boston, George Washington dug his quill pen into the paper as he begged each man to stay until new recruits arrived. He knew that the Second Continental Congress had encouraged men to enlist for only a year since they thought the war would be over soon. Now, many of those men had left for home. After Lexington and Concord, thousands of northern militiamen besieged Boston, pushing General William Howe back and penning him within the narrow city limits. Morale sank low since the earlier American retreat at Bunker (Breed's) Hill.

Washington, overseeing the Siege of Boston since April 19, 1775, desperately wanted to take Boston back from the British, but he had few men and little ammunition to break the stalemate. In early February, Washington discussed the possibility of stationing heavy artillery on the strategic hills south of Boston called Dorchester Heights, in order to threaten the harbor which held the British Royal

Colonel Knox bringing cannons from Fort Ticonderoga

Navy commanded by Admiral Molyneux Shuldham. But the local Council of Safety objected, stating that Howe had too many troops and the Continentals too little gunpowder to attempt to take the Heights.

At last, Colonel Henry Knox suggested using the cannons, mortars, and ammunition captured by Ethan Allen and his Green Mountain Boys at Fort Ticonderoga in New York and Crown Point on Lake Champlain in 1775. But the badly-needed supplies lay hundreds of miles away over poor roads. When Washington agreed to let him try, Colonel Knox set out on a journey that would demonstrate his brilliant logistical abilities. When he reached the north, Knox and his men shoved the heavy cannons onto boats and ferries, tied them to ox-drawn sledges and dragged them painfully along rough winter roads through the lonely Berkshire Mountains. For three months, they navigated two partially-frozen rivers and wound through forests and swamps.

Nearing the Boston area, Colonel Knox skimmed over the snow towards Cambridge. He drove in with eighty sleds packed with the giant shapes of captured cannons, mortars, and heavy artillery. Washington, looking over the tens of thousands of pounds of new artillery that Knox brought, decided to act immediately. Since two thousand of his nine thousand men had no muskets, the general ordered his armed troops to fire into Boston from the west during the night of March 2nd-3rd.

General Washington positioning troops and cannons

He stationed some of his heavy cannons at Cobble Hill and Lechmere's Point in Cambridge, while he placed a third battery on Lamb's Dam in the town of Roxbury. While soldiers prepared to move more artillery to the Heights, Washington kept up a steady fire on the British, who fired back all night. The barrage, while continuous, resulted in few casualties on either side. Eight hundred Continental soldiers stood on guard along the river near Dorchester, protecting the shore while cannons again boomed through the night on March 2, as soldiers assembled materials to build earthwork defenses against the British above Boston Harbor.

When the sun went down on March 4th, the thunder and red glow of Washington's cannons gave his soldiers the signal to take the Heights. General John Thomas, leading the two thousand troops who had no muskets, climbed silently to the top of Dorchester Heights under cover of darkness. Some carried trenching tools or drove ox-drawn wagons piled with hay. Others hauled along spare cannon equipment. They moved through the foggy night that shrouded the foot of the hill. As they emerged from the haze, the men found the hilltop providentially flooded with clear silver moonlight. Working feverishly under the cold spring moon, the soldiers stacked hay on the ground between them and the harbor to muffle the noise of their work. Fresh troops constantly reinforced the tired soldiers during the night, dragging cannons to posts looking out on the harbor, and throwing up dirt from earthworks overlooking the sleeping town of Boston.

All night, General Washington moved up and down the line, his quiet, steady voice encouraging

British General William Howe

the men. Tomorrow, he reminded them, was the sixth anniversary of the Boston Massacre. At 4 a.m., the exhausted soldiers straightened their backs to view their work. Earth fortifications rose like shadows in the pale dawn, their walls strong enough to withstand both pistol fire and grapeshot. But the men did not stop. Work crews chopped down trees to construct a formidable abatis of sharpened tree trunks jutting outward like teeth to slow down the British attacking the position. On the outside of the defenses, the soldiers placed barrels filled with rocks that looked like part of the earthworks. But soldiers could roll these heavy barrels downhill into the rows of attacking Redcoats.

On the morning of March 4, General Howe awoke to find Continental cannons directed towards his troops from Dorchester Heights. Astonished, he exclaimed: "The rebels have done more in one night than my whole army could do in months." In fact, Washington's troops had worked for two nights straight, careful to conceal their first night's work from British eyes.

View of Boston from Dorchester Heights

As a shrewd military commander, Washington knew that Howe would either evacuate his troops or try to storm the hill. He believed that Howe would realize that this line of attack had unpleasant

General Howe supervises the evacuation of British troops from Boston

similarities to the Battle of Bunker Hill, which resulted in enormous British losses. Washington decided to strike at Boston from the direction of Cambridge if Howe launched an attack on Dorchester Heights. In preparation, he arranged two floating artillery batteries. In addition to these, he organized a fleet of boats that could hold nearly three thousand soldiers.

Worried, Admiral Shuldham informed Howe that every moment Washington held Dorchester Heights increased the navy's danger. Washington had accurately inferred Howe's mind. Meeting with his staff in an emergency council-of-war, the British commander considered his options and decided to take twenty-four hundred men and assault the Heights under cover of darkness. Meanwhile, Washington's spies informed him of Howe's plans. The General responded by strengthening his troops on the Heights until almost six thousand Continentals stood holding the line in the cold darkness. Below in the harbor, Howe turned his cannons aboard his ships to aim at the patriots on the hill.

As the poorly-dressed Continental soldiers waited for the British regulars to attack, a sudden savage snowstorm blew up on the night of March 5th. The surprising violent blizzard hit the British ships, knocking them together, splintering their masts, and destroying the fighting power of the British fleet. Nearby, in the town of Roxbury, the Reverend William Gordon felt a chill when he heard the wind roaring in the treetops and thought of the Continental Army. "When I heard in the night how amazingly strong the wind blew," he recalled, "I pleased myself with the reflection that the Lord might be working delivery for us and thus prevent the diffusion of human blood."

Gordon was right. Next morning, Howe saw his destroyed fleet huddled together in the harbor under the swirling snowflakes. Realizing that he would have no time to repair the damage before the

Americans attacked, Howe decided not to launch a costly counteroffensive against Washington's superior forces. He backed off, preferring to preserve his troops for combat instead of holding onto Boston. When the snow stopped on March 8th, British intermediaries appeared at Washington's camp with an unsigned document. In it, the British assured Washington that they would not burn Boston if the Continental Army allowed Howe's ten thousand troops to leave quietly. Hampered by stormy weather, the Redcoats finally evacuated Boston by sea on March 17, 1776. They sailed out of the colonies for New York and Halifax, Nova Scotia, where they hoped to control both the city and the traffic to and from Canada. With them sailed more than a thousand Loyalist citizens.

That same day, the victorious Continental Army marched into Boston. At this point, not a single British soldier existed anywhere in the thirteen colonies. Washington later wrote to Gordon that "Providence ... conducted us through difficulties where no human foresight could point the way." Following the miraculous victory at Dorchester Heights, Continental troops maintained the fortifications on the hill until they abandoned them at the end of the war.

Washington and his troops demonstrated valor in their plan to occupy Dorchester Heights, a move that resulted in the temporary evacuation of all British troops from American shores.

Questions

1. What did Washington propose to end the Siege of Boston?
2. What did Henry Knox suggest to help accomplish that goal?
3. What difficulties did Knox and his men encounter making the plan a reality?
4. How did Washington implement his plan?
5. What providential occurrence aided the building of earthworks?
6. Of what event did Washington remind his men to encourage them?
7. What was the plan for the barrels on the outside of the defenses?
8. What was General Howe's comment when he observed what the patriots had accomplished in two nights?
9. What was Howe's plan of attack?
10. What second providential occurrence happened to aid the patriots?
11. What was Reverend Gordon's account of what happened?

12. How did it happen that 10,000 British troops evacuated Boston without the loss of blood?
13. What did Washington write to Reverend Gordon?

Attentiveness

DEFINITION

Giving care or attention;
watchful, alertness

MEMORY VERSE

Watch ye, stand fast in the faith,
quit you like men, be strong.

I Corinthians 16:13

Poisoned Peas

Samuel Fraunces

New York City

June 22–28, 1776

He did not expect to find poison in the food today. Fifty-four-year-old "Black Sam" strolled through the rooms of his tavern standing solidly at the juncture of New York City's Pearl and Dock Streets. The usual rousing atmosphere, rich with food, voices, and laughter, greeted him. People never knew where Fraunces picked up the nickname "Black Sam." Listed by an early census as a "Free White," "Black Sam" might have referred to the dark brown eyes under his curled white wig or to a hot temper. Two years earlier, the New York Sons of Liberty had crowded into Fraunces' Tavern. The air thickened with plotting. Heads bent over tables, the men discussed their plan. Then they slipped out of the tavern and out to the waterfront where they dumped expensive crates of East Indian tea into the Hudson River and watched them sink. As the British filtered into New York, more and more Redcoat officers would appear at "Black Sam's" tavern, humming into their cups as they drank at his tables. Once, a cannonball fired by the British warship *Asia* out in the harbor crashed through the tavern's roof.

He could expect General George Washington today. With his headquarters at Richmond Hill, just two miles up the street to the north, Washington and his officers often rode down to Fraunces' tavern to get a bite to eat and relax in the stimulating atmosphere. Today, Fraunces walked through his tavern as usual, supervising the dishes that came and went, following up on orders for catering services, and testing the wines. Colorful bottles of nuts, soup, preserved fruit, pickled vegetables, oysters, ketchup, fresh jellies, and mouth-watering marmalades crowded on shelves. One of his slaves scurried through the busy tavern. Gentlemen with powdered hair, embroidered coats, and knee breeches sat in rooms glimmering with candlelight. A party with music and dancing filled another of the tavern's chambers. Sometimes men met secretly at Fraunces' Tavern to whisper and plan. During the daytime, the New York Provincial Congress rented out several rooms as office space. Tired visitors, having supped a fixed-price dinner, could totter off to fall into bed in one of the inn's five lodging rooms available.

Today, George Washington arrived as usual and took a seat near one of the windows. Meanwhile, one of Washington's men crept up to an unknown thirteen-year-old girl nicknamed Phoebe. Having begun a little romance with Phoebe, he confessed that the New York Loyalists had bribed him to lace Washington's green peas with a fatal dose of arsenic. Phoebe, attentive to the impending danger, watched for her chance to warn Washington.

Fraunces' Tavern, New York City, 1776

No one quite knew what happened next. Phoebe may have warned Fraunces about the plot. The plate of food with the green peas arrived, and Washington started to eat. Suddenly, Phoebe snatched the plate from Washington and threw it out the window. The chickens outside scrambled to gobble up the peas. Six died on the spot. Blame initially fell on a drummer boy named William Greene and a fifer, James Johnson. Twenty or more people were arrested that week and then released.

Washington in the tavern, saying farewell at the end of the war

Meanwhile, a man by the name of Sergeant Thomas Hickey sat in a dingy New York City prison, far away from the scene of his supposed crime. As a member of the "Commander-in-Chief's Lifeguard," Hickey was responsible for Washington's safety. He also kept track of the General's official papers and a store of cash belonging to the Continental Army. Arrested on June 15, 1776, for counterfeiting money, Hickey found himself behind solid walls. While in prison, worn out with boredom, Hickey confessed to his fellow prisoner Isaac Ketchum that he and a larger ring of Continental soldiers planned to run away and join the British as soon as they landed in New York. His name was suspected as being involved in the plot to poison Washington. His loose tongue sealed Hickey's fate. He suddenly went from small-time counterfeiter to world-class traitor. Handed over to the Continental Army, he faced four witnesses, including the drummer William Greene, who accused him of mutiny.

Rumors continued to run wild through New York City, ballooning out of proportion as the stories escalated to include attempts to kidnap Washington and General Israel Putnam, kill his officers, and blow up the arsenals belonging to the Continental Army. Finally, trembling from the rumors and their sense of escape from unknown plotters, the New York Provincial Congress joyfully held a celebratory dinner at Fraunces Tavern. They offered well wishes, over thirty-one in all, for the safety of Washington and his army.

The legend of the poisoned peas continues to intrigue American history lovers more than two hundred years later. Digging deeper, historians have not been able to fully uncover all the details, but certain facts remain. In a letter to Congress, dated March 5, 1785, Samuel Fraunces begged for a pension, claiming to have foiled a plot to kill Washington in 1776. While Congress did grant Fraunces a stipend, the letter gives no clues as to the nature of the attempted crime. The story of the poisoned peas first appeared in the *Poughkeepsie Journal* on March 14, 1832. The article divulged the exciting story during the enthusiastic celebration of George Washington's 100th birthday. Although it claims that "Black Sam" saved Washington's life, it fails to mention any Phoebe. Then in 1859, the famous historian, Benson J. Lossing, inserted the story in his notes to Custis' memoirs. He claimed that the daughter of innkeeper Samuel Fraunces discovered the plot, but he did not give her name.

Samuel Fraunces claimed to have actually saved George Washington's life in 1776. What is clear from the historical record is that Hickey, arrested for counterfeiting money, was turned over to the Continental Army and court-martialed on charges of mutiny and treason. The trial records mentioned no attempt on his part to poison General Washington. He pleaded not guilty to all charges. At 11 o'clock on the morning of June 28, 1776, a crowd gathered on a field east of the Bowery to witness his execution. Hickey walked to the scaffold before the eyes of 20,000 soldiers and civilians. Any soldier present who had considered deserting to General Howe would have thought twice before risking his neck. As they put the noose around Hickey's neck, Reverend Jacob Corwin, standing near the scaffold, heard Hickey mutter something against William Greene—the drummer who testified against him. Hickey was the first person hanged for treason early on in the Revolutionary War, and the first person executed for treason against the future United States of America. Washington, years later, requested "Black Sam" to become his personal steward at his New York residence when he was elected president.

A dark plot had ended in the loss of a treacherous life, and a noble life had been saved through the watchful attentiveness of a humble tavern worker.

....I shall rely therefore, confidently, on that Providence which has heretofore preserved, & been bountiful to me, not doubting but that I shall return safe to you in the fall—I shall feel no pain from the Toil, or the danger of the Campaign—My unhappiness will flow, from the uneasiness I know you will feel at being left alone—I therefore beg of you to summon your whole fortitude & Resolution....

—George Washington

Questions

1. What kind of business did Samuel Fraunces run?
2. Why was Washington coming to the tavern?
3. What plot had been conceived against Washington?
4. Whose attentiveness alerted others to danger?
5. What did Phoebe do to save General Washington?
6. Who was suspected as being instrumental in planning this treachery?
7. What did Hickey confess to?
8. What are some ways in which you can practice attentiveness to danger in your life?

Persuasiveness

DEFINITION

Skillfully handling truth to lead others in a right path

MEMORY VERSE

And the servant of the Lord must not strive; but be gentle unto all men, apt to teach, patient . . .

II Timothy 2:24

The Mentor

Rev. John Witherspoon

Philadelphia, Pennsylvania

July 2, 1776

As he glanced around the crowded assembly room of the Second Continental Congress at No. 500 Chestnut Street, president of Princeton John Witherspoon saw the faces of his former students. Some of them, like James Madison, Aaron Burr Jr., and delegates from Delaware, New Jersey, Maryland, Virginia, and North Carolina were present. They sat like eager pupils at small tables with wooden Windsor chairs, their faces flushed with excitement. The air buzzed with the clamor of their voices. But they were not discussing Latin grammar or arguing an obscure point of philosophy. As relations with Great Britain deteriorated and British troops invaded New Jersey and the other northern colonies, they knew that the time had come to vote for more negotiation or for independence.

Reverend John Witherspoon

Heavyset, with pink cheeks and a wispy white wig, fifty-three-year-old John Witherspoon had come as a New Jersey delegate to vote on the Virginia Resolution for Independence. As he looked around the hall, he realized he was also the only college president present that day.

Debate raged around him. The delegates could not make up their minds to take the dreaded step and actually confront Britain with a call for independence. They knew that it would mean total war. Their decision today would put their wives and children, their property, and even their lives at extreme risk. They argued, then adjourned, then argued again. The steamy dispute continued into the night and resumed the next day. As he listened, John Witherspoon knew that they had to arrive at a deciding vote. As far as he was concerned, there could be only one answer to that vote.

Finally, one member stood up and begged for them to adopt a cautious approach towards Britain. He protested that the time for revolution was not ripe yet. Suddenly, John Witherspoon rose to his full height, his white hair gleaming. "The time," he exclaimed, "is far past ripe. In fact, it is rotten."

His voice shook with emotion. "There is a tide in the affairs of man, a nick of time; we perceive it now before us. The noble instrument upon your table, which insures immortality to its author, should be subscribed this very morning by every pen in the House. He who will not respond to its accents, and strain every nerve to carry into effect its provisions, is unworthy of the name of freeman."

The room became deadly quiet.

John Witherspoon raised his voice and continued. "For my own part, of property I have some, of reputation more. That reputation is staked, that property is pledged, on the issue of this context; and although these gray hairs must soon descend into the sepulcher, I would infinitely rather they should descend thither by the hand of the public executioner than desert, at this crisis, the sacred cause of my country."

Signing of the Declaration of Independence, July 4, 1776

Many of these men had heard this white-haired college president and minister's voice echo through the halls of Princeton. They had listened to his pragmatic Scottish teaching. Their minds had been sculpted by this craftsman of words and ideologies.

Then Witherspoon finished speaking. As he sat down, worn with emotion, a heavy sigh of relief rustled through the room like autumn leaves falling from the trees. Voices murmured in approval as the tension, hesitation, and paralyzing fear regarding the outcome of their decision blew away in a fresh wind of patriotism. Each member knew that he was not alone. Everyone there was risking his life, his family, and everything he owned. If the rebellion failed, they could be branded as traitors and shipped to England for trial. Benjamin Franklin spoke up wryly: "Gentlemen, we must all hang together or assuredly we shall all hang separately." John Witherspoon's speech carried the day as all fifty-five delegates to the Continental Congress rose in a wave of enthusiasm and pledged their lives, property, and honor to the fight against Great Britain.

In the future, John Witherspoon would sit on more than one hundred twenty Congressional committees. These included the Committee on Secret Correspondence of Foreign Affairs, the Board of War, and the Committee on Clothing for the Army. His work on the War Committee, raising funds to keep the Continental troops in the field, often brought him into close contact with George Washington. Later, he would help to draft the Articles of Confederation.

During his twenty-six years as president of Princeton, Witherspoon graduated four hundred seventy-eight students. Most of these would have a direct influence on the founding of America. One of his students, James Madison, who later served as the first Secretary of State, constructed many of the fundamentals of the United States' Constitution. Aaron Burr, Jr., went on to become a vice-president. Three United States Supreme Court Justices, ten cabinet members, twenty-one senators, thirty-nine U.S. representatives, twenty-one state governors, one hundred fourteen ministers and nine of the fifty-five delegates to the Constitutional Convention graduated from Princeton under John Witherspoon's mentorship.

Two months before the vote for independence, the Continental Congress declared a national day of fasting, humiliation, and prayer. That day, John Witherspoon preached a sermon to a hall of students at Princeton University. In his closing words, the great minister and college president summed up his worldview on religion and the revolution in a few persuasive words:

"It is in the man of piety and inward principle, that we may expect to find the uncorrupted patriot, the useful citizen, and the invincible soldier."

John Witherspoon's compelling speech on the floor of the Continental Congress turned the day in favor of a vote for independence from England. John

Witherspoon's influence on the founding fathers and his persuasiveness at an hour of crisis made a lasting impact on America.

God grant that in America true religion and civil liberty may be inseparable and that the unjust attempts to destroy the one, may in the issue tend to the support and establishment of both.

—Reverend John Witherspoon

Questions

1. Who were some of Witherspoon's former students?
2. Why was the decision for independence so widely disputed?
3. What was Witherspoon's famous quote when one delegate proclaimed the time was not yet ripe for revolution?
4. What did he say that made the men in the room fall silent?
5. What was Benjamin Franklin's comment?
6. How many students would Witherspoon influence?
7. Read again Witherspoon's words preached in a sermon to a hall of students at Princeton University.
8. How did Witherspoon's compelling speech at the Continental Congress persuade others to join the cause for liberty?

Responsibility

DEFINITION

Doing my best at every task assigned to me because God is watching and I want to do my best for Him

MEMORY VERSE

So then every one of us shall give account of himself to God.

Romans 14:12

Silver Tongue

Richard Henry Lee

Philadelphia, Pennsylvania
June 7, 1776

He rose, in the room's sudden hush, staring straight towards the Congressional president's chair. Tall and slim, with an aristocratic face, forty-four-year-old Richard Henry Lee looked pale and ill. The fifty-six delegates to the Second Continental Congress shifted in their chairs to get a better look as the famous orator opened his mouth. Despite his years in Virginia, Lee's voice still carried the clipped intonations of his English education.

The other members knew him well. In 1774, as

a delegate to the First Continental Congress, Lee pushed for the non-importation of British goods. In addition, he worked tirelessly to select and then win support for George Washington as Commander-in-Chief of the Continental Army, even convincing Massachusetts cousins Samuel and John Adams to accept the Virginian. Working with Patrick Henry and Thomas Jefferson, Lee had proved instrumental in forming the Virginia Committee of Correspondence that kept the colonies informed of British actions.

By the early summer of 1776, war with Britain seemed imminent. Already, Hessian troops appeared on American shores, enraging many colonists. The battles of Lexington and Concord convinced some of the impossibility of reconciliation, while the majority of colonists did not favor independence from England. Many in Congress believed in the 1775 Olive Branch Petition, submitted to Parliament the year before as a final bid for peace. Meanwhile, Thomas Paine's recently-published *Common Sense,* attacking the concept of the monarchy, urged people towards independence.

On May 15th, the Virginia Convention, meeting in Williamsburg, took the first step towards independence. The war, as Patrick Henry pointed out, had already begun at Lexington and Concord. Other patriot victories in Massachusetts and along Lake Champlain proved peace with Great Britain was impossible. Edmund Pendleton, the President of the Virginia Convention, chose Richard Henry Lee to make the move for independence before the Continental Congress.

Now, Lee raised his hand, wrapped in black silk to hide the fingers crushed and mangled from a

Richard Henry Lee
(portrait showing his wrapped hand)

hunting accident. Sweeping his hand in a dramatic gesture, Lee argued "that these United Colonies are, and of right ought to be, free and independent States, that they are absolved from all allegiance to the British Crown, and that all political connection between them and the State of Great Britain is, and ought to be, totally dissolved."

As Lee stopped speaking, John Adams spoke up. The round little delegate from Massachusetts

The Committee of Five

seconded Lee's motion. Despite the show of support, many members of Congress felt uncomfortable with Lee's resolution. The delegates from the northern colonies, such as New York, Delaware, New Jersey, Maryland, and Pennsylvania knew that they did not have the authority to vote for independence without their local governments' consent. John Hancock, as president of Congress, agreed to let the delegates postpone Lee's resolution for three weeks. During that time, the men from the northern colonies set to work to gain support among the colonial governments for independence.

Meanwhile, on June 11th, a "Committee of Five" wasted no time in drawing up a formal declaration of independence. With Lee's words, quoted almost verbatim from the Virginia Convention, in mind, Thomas Jefferson spent those three hot summer weeks hard at work crafting the Declaration of Independence. The other members of the group included John Adams from Massachusetts, Benjamin Franklin from Pennsylvania, and Roger Sherman of Connecticut.

June 28, 1776, arrived. The northern delegates, back from their labors, returned to their seats in the Congress hall. They listened as the "Committee of Five" presented their declaration, and explained their reasons for it, to the assembly. First, they called for a complete and final break with Great Britain. Next, they declared the importance of forming foreign alliances, particularly with England's traditional enemies, France and Spain. Finally, they wanted to form a confederation government to see the country through a foreseeable time of war. Unlike a republican form of government, with divided powers, a confederation existed on a weak level, with only nominal authority and an inability to enforce taxes. Like his fellow Virginian, Thomas Jefferson, Lee believed in small government. "The first maxim of a man who loves liberty," Lee argued, "should be never to grant to rulers an atom of power that is not most clearly and indispensably necessary for the safety and well being of society."

But Lee's eloquent resolution still had not convinced everyone. Voices broke out in agreement, some in opposition. Some felt that they still ought to try to smooth things out with Parliament. Others still needed support and confirmation from their home governments. The debate raged for several days. Congress wanted the decision to be unanimous, either all for independence or all against it.

Finally, on July 2nd, twelve of the thirteen colonies, New York abstaining, voted to adopt Lee's Resolution. This done, Congress moved ahead to consider the Declaration of Independence. Congress worked for the next two-and-a-half days, scrutinizing the document, deleting some paragraphs and altering others.

During the late morning of July 4, 1776, the Second Continental Congress officially adopted the Declaration of Independence. The meeting over, the "Committee of Five" rushed to take the manuscript copy of the declaration document over to John

Richard Henry Lee

Dunlap, who worked as official printer for Congress. After the first flush of excitement, the actual signing of the Declaration of Independence did not happen all at once. While a number of members signed on July 4th, heartily echoing Lee's resolution, most members did not sign until August 2nd. Richard Henry Lee, along with northern delegates Elbridge Gerry and Oliver Wolcott, waited until September 4th to set their names to the document. The last two members did not sign until 1781.

Although later overshadowed by the Declaration of Independence, the *Pennsylvania Evening Post* announced Lee's eloquent and determined Resolution on the evening of July 2nd:

"This day the Continental Congress declared the United Colonies Free and Independent States."

Richard Henry Lee demonstrated responsibility by carrying out the instructions of the Virginia Convention and urging the Second Continental Congress towards independence.

Questions

1. Tell how the colonists had lawfully appealed to King George III on numerous occasions.
2. What did Lee present in his resolution to Congress?
3. Who seconded his motion?
4. Why was the vote postponed?
5. Which men were included in the "Committee of Five" to draw up the Declaration of Independence?
6. When was the resolution adopted?
7. How did Richard Henry Lee demonstrate responsibility?
8. Think of ways you can demonstrate responsibility in your home.

Resourcefulness

DEFINITION

Using things which others might discard in a creative way

MEMORY VERSE

He that is faithful in that which is least is faithful also in much: and he that is unjust in the least is unjust also in much.

Luke 16:10

His Melted Majesty

Oliver Wolcott

Litchfield, Connecticut

July 9, 1776

As his coach bounced over the dusty roads, fifty-year-old Connecticut delegate General Oliver Wolcott knew that he had just made one of the greatest decisions of his life. A short time before in Philadelphia, he had scribbled his name on the bottom of a document that announced the American colonies' intention to free themselves from the control of King George III and Great Britain. Today in New York, General George Washington picked up a copy of the new Declaration of Independence. Then his voice rolled out over the troops' heads.

Sons of Liberty pulling down the statue of King George III

> "The history of the present King of Great Britain is a history of repeated injuries and usurpations, all having in direct object the establishment of an absolute Tyranny over these States … He has plundered our seas, ravaged our Coasts, burnt our towns, and destroyed the lives of our people."

As Washington finished speaking, whoops and cheers broke out. That same night, forty soldiers, sailors, and citizens, led by Captain Oliver Brown and the Sons of Liberty, rushed towards the Bowling

Green, situated at the tip of Manhattan. Looming above them in the summer twilight stood the 4,000-pound lead statue of King George III, fashioned in 1771 by London sculptor Joseph Wilton. The monarch straddled a horse atop a heavy marble base surrounded by an iron fence below. Staring coldly into the distance, King George III wore flowing Roman robes painted with gilt. Someone threw a rope over George's head. It slipped down over the horse's body. When they all pulled together, the rope broke. They threw another rope and it caught and held. Suddenly, the statue hurtled to the ground with an earth-shaking crash. The king's head snapped off as it hit the ground and rolled to the feet of the patriots.

The Sons of Liberty wanted to hoist the statue's head onto a pike and wave it aloft as they marched through the city. But during the confusion that night, New York Tories stole the statue's head and shipped it back to London. It served as a grim warning that must have reverberated through British minds as a reminder of the death of Charles I at the end of the English Civil War.

When Oliver Wolcott, on his way home from Philadelphia and New York, learned of the monarch's trunk, he secretly brought it home to Litchfield, Connecticut. Wolcott moved so quickly and silently that the statue disappeared before the Tories could locate it. In Litchfield, Wolcott's Tory neighbors,

David Sloan and Job Burlock, who hid British agents in his house, knew that something was afoot when an ox cart arrived at Wolcott's house and deposited a large bundle. Sounds of a hammer broke out from Wolcott's backyard as he hastily built a shed in the center of the apple orchard. Just across the street, Tory neighbor Samuel Belden spied on Wolcott from his store window. But the apple trees' thick green foliage successfully camouflaged the shed

General Oliver Wolcott

from prying eyes. Inside the small shed, Oliver Wolcott picked up a hatchet he normally used for chopping wood. Bringing it down on the soft lead, he began breaking apart the statue, passing the chunks to his wife, fifteen-year-old daughter Laura, eleven-year-old daughter Marianne, and nine-year-old son Frederick.

Molten lead pouring into a bullet mold

lead bullets

Inside the house, excitement ran high. Stooping over the glowing red coals in the great kitchen fireplace, Wolcott's wife, children, and three neighbor women melted down the lumps of lead. Then they poured the lead into bullet molds. Despite the hot kitchen, the children shivered with a sense of desperate secrecy. For them, melting down King George's statue became a "frolic." Laughter and jokes flew through the air. If the British mercenaries were so determined to fight for the King, they ought to have "melted majesty fired at them." In spite of the fun, the women and children realized what this amount of ammunition could mean to a new army often running low on bullets. Slaving over the hot fire and dangerous lead splatters, Laura made 8,378 bullets in a day. Marianne topped her sister with 10,790 bullets and their small brother Frederick added his 936 cartridges to the pile. By the end of the day, King George III had yielded 42,088 bullets for the patriot cause. But the Wolcotts had not finished. Over one-third of the lead still sat in the shed. Meanwhile, every moment that they held onto the statue increased their personal danger. Sometime during the night, threatened by their Tory neighbors who determined to sabotage the operation, Wolcott and his family had to stop casting bullets.

Under cover of darkness, they lugged statue pieces across the road to the swamp. Standing at the edge, they hurled the heavy chunks into the Davis Swamp and watched them sink. Then they took shovels out at night and buried King George's left arm, a piece of his thigh, bits of the saddle and gilded coat skirt from the statue. Some fourteen hundred pounds of the Wilton's George III statue disappeared without being melted down into bullets. Years later, they would emerge again as farmers turned up chunks of lead with their plow blades during spring planting.

Oliver Wolcott, realizing how desperately the Continental Army needed ammunition, loaded up his 42,000 bullets and transported them to the nearly empty military arsenal. When the Litchfield Militia responded to a British alarm, Wolcott split up his ammunition, giving fifty cartridges to the militiamen and three hundred bullets to Colonel Edward Wigglesworth. Wolcott kept careful notes and receipts about these transactions, demonstrating how valuable the northern colonists considered ammunition. The melted monarch came into his full glory a year later during the Battle of Saratoga in September–October 1777. General Oliver Wolcott, commanding a brigade of Connecticut militia, sent a hail of homemade lead into the British ranks, shooting them down with "hot blasts of His Melted Majesty." In the heat of battle, Wolcott's militiamen captured "Gentleman Johnny" Burgoyne, ending the conflict. The defeat of the British army at Saratoga would convince the French, who had previously hovered on the edge of an American alliance, to assist the colonies against Britain.

Oliver Wolcott, signer of the Declaration of Independence and later Governor of Connecticut, demonstrated resourcefulness by using the resources he had at hand to create ammunition that proved valuable to the American cause.

Questions

1. What was one of the greatest decisions of Oliver Wolcott's life?
2. What did he witness in New York as George Washington read aloud the Declaration of Independence?
3. How many pounds did King George's statue weigh? What was it made from?
4. What decision did Wolcott make as he planned his return to Connecticut?
5. What did Wolcott do with the statue?
7. How many bullets did Laura make? Marianne? Frederick?
8. How may bullets had been made by the end of the day?
9. Why were the Wolcotts in danger?
10. What did they do with the remaining chunks of the statue?
11. Where did General Wolcott use many of the bullets a year later?
12. Tell why this is such a good example of resourcefulness?
13. Think of something you might use for a good purpose which might otherwise be discarded.

We hold these truths to be self-evident, that all men are created equal, that they are endowed by their Creator with certain unalienable Rights, that among these are Life, Liberty and the pursuit of Happiness.–That to secure these rights, Governments are instituted among Men, deriving their just powers from the consent of the governed...

—The Declaration of Independence, August 2nd, 1776

Honesty

DEFINITION

Speaking the truth in all situations

MEMORY VERSE

Wherefore putting away lying, speak every man truth with his neighbour: for we are members one of another.

Ephesians 4:25

The Hunted

John Hart

Hopewell, New Jersey
Winter, 1776

He crouched at the edge of the farmlands, among the stubble of winter crops, peering through the rime-whitened trees at the burned-out gristmill, orchards, and barns. Only the stone house had not burned. Sixty-three-year-old John Hart shivered, hugging his slender body, his grey-shot dark hair whipping in the wind as he stared towards the home where he had lived with Deborah for almost forty years. He could not think of her now. If he did, he would see her lying in that bed again, white and ill, looking at him with those beautiful eyes—the same eyes that he had ridden thirty miles on horseback just to have a glimpse of so long ago. Shivering in the cold wind, John Hart had no idea where his twelve children had gone, the older boys and girls, or the little ones. They had vanished while he was gone, as surely as the skeletons of his horses, cattle,

"Honest" John Hart

pigs, sheep, and chickens lay scattered under the snow. Hart stared towards the vanished paradise like a wild animal, as if he would suddenly see a wisp of grey smoke rising from the chimney or his wife appear in the doorway with the warmth of the fire and the laughter of children behind her. But he knew that he would never see it again.

In December 1776, Washington's battered army had retreated across the length of New Jersey. In their wake, Hessian mercenaries, with tricorn hats and pointed brass helmets over their tarry pigtails, swept through the Hopewell countryside, looting and burning patriot properties. The last time he saw this place, smoke rose from the countryside. His children scattered, running into the fields as Hessian troops moved in to torch the outbuildings and slaughter the livestock. Inside the house, John Hart knelt by his wife's side as she lay too ill to move in bed. Finally, as the troops approached the house to take him prisoner, John Hart let go of his wife's hand and escaped into the forest. He knew that they would treat the sick woman more gently if her patriot husband had left. As it grew dark, with the taste of snow in the air, John Hart slipped away to hide in a nearby natural rock formation known as the Rock House.

Making his way to a sheltered cave sandwiched between trees and rocks, he ducked inside, hunkering down against the cold. Always on the run, often hiding somewhere on the six hundred acres of his homestead plantation, John Hart managed to keep watch over his destroyed property during the long course of the Revolutionary War. As the war swept through New Jersey, John Hart fled to the Sourland Mountains, rising cold and bleak above the wasted landscape. Hiding in a series of caves among the bare foliage in winter, he watched the seasons pass and change in the valley. Leaves floated down, making way for deep snow that made it hard to survive. Spring turned the ground moist, giving way to bird songs and summer. Hunger often tore at his insides. Once, on the run, he had no place to sleep. Instead, he lay down beside a large dog, sharing its warmth. For a time, the dog proved John Hart's only friend. And still he could not go home.

When he placed his name on the Declaration of Independence as a delegate to the New Jersey Provincial Congress, John Hart never dreamed of the hardships which that decision would cost him. Known as "Honest John," Hart served his country in a variety of ways, both as a signer personally responsible for the "Bill of Credit Notes," cash issued by the new State of New Jersey, and as Speaker of the General Assembly. Under similar pressure from the British, Hart's friend, Samuel Tucker, the President of the Joint Meeting of the New Jersey legislature, signed an oath of allegiance to the British crown in exchange for the promise of amnesty.

Not until Washington crossed the Delaware, striking the British and Hessians (German soldiers who fought for the British) at Trenton and Princeton, in January of 1777, could John Hart return to his cold and empty hearthstone. With his health broken from years of semi-starvation and surviving the winters and summers in the mountains, the sixty-five-year-old man began repairing the ruins of his farm. Before the war, he had owned hundreds of acres, a gristmill, and large numbers of livestock. He had a wife and children. Now, he was penniless, in poor health, and had no idea where his children

Sourland Mountain boulders like those among which John Hart might have hidden.

had gone. By some accounts, he would never see any of his children again.

June came, and with it the mutterings of a coming battle. On June 22nd, Hart asked the Continental Army to camp in the fields on his farm. Twelve thousand American soldiers set up their rifles and started cooking fires on Hart's property. Washington ate lunch with the signer of the Declaration of Independence before withdrawing to the nearby Hunt House nearby for a council of war in preparation to fight the Battle of Monmouth less than a week later. The battle ended in a draw, leading to a long-term victory for Washington's troops. Following the battle of Princeton, the elderly John Hart enlisted as a private in the Continental Army, on top of his duties in the General Assembly. Five months later, John Hart staggered home from his work in the Assembly at Trenton, suffering severe pain from "gravel" or kidney stones. Two days later, he could not take to the road in order to return to his duties. By May 11, 1779, his body, weakened by the hardships of the Revolution, gave out completely. He slipped away at age sixty-eight in the home he had built long ago for Deborah and where they had raised twelve children.

A plain Presbyterian farmer with little education, "Honest John Hart" gave his "life, fortune, and sacred honor" for the sake of liberty. Even though he died before the end of the war, "he never repented the course he had taken. He enlisted himself in a good cause; and in the darkest periods, still believed that a righteous Providence would ultimately enable that cause to prevail, and finally to triumph."

Our Constitution was made only for a moral and religious People. It is wholly inadequate to the government of any other.

—John Adams

Questions

1. For what character quality was John Hart known?
2. Why did John Hart have to flee from his home?
3. How many children did John have?
4. How did Hart manage to stay warm on a cold winter night?
5. When was Hart able to return home?
6. What state did he find his farm and family in?
7. How did John Hart continue working for the cause of freedom after returning home?
8. Would people think of you as an honest person?

Diligence

DEFINITION

Viewing each task given to me as
a special duty and putting forth the
effort to do my very best

MEMORY VERSE

He becometh poor that dealeth with
a slack hand: but the hand of the
diligent maketh rich.
He that gathereth in summer is a
wise son: but he that sleepeth in
harvest is a son that causeth shame.

Proverbs 10:4–5

Christmas Crossing

Col. John Glover & the Marblehead Men

Trenton, New Jersey

December 24–25, 1776

Snow fell on the Delaware. The flakes came thickly, softly, threatening to hide the landscape from the Continental soldiers' eyes. The boat bumped as it scraped against the broad sheets of ice coating the Delaware. Freezing rain beat down on the Commander-in-Chief, George Washington, and the men as they huddled in the rocking boats. Only the tough Marblehead Men, used to the bitter fishing off the coast of Massachusetts, rowed steadily ahead. Crouched in the boat with his men, forty-four-year-old Colonel John Glover wore a tight, white-and-blue uniform under his woolen greatcoat. The wind whipped his wavy hair gathered at the back of his neck as he checked the brace of silver pistols he wore at his belt. A basket-hilted Scottish broadsword hung at his side. A sturdy seaman from Marblehead, Massachusetts, the colonel had little doubt that his men would reach the opposite shore. He had seen worse weather as a ship owner and merchant. Now, as commander of the 14th Marblehead Militia or "Glover's Regiment," he saw to it that his rugged sailors could handle oars as well as muskets.

Swelled with the recent British victory in New York, the Hessians on the other side of the Delaware River in Trenton, New Jersey, relaxed to celebrate Christmas Eve. They ate, drank, and partied late into the night. Sentries, dulled to their surroundings and sheltering from the sleet, would not watch the shore closely. Washington knew that he had to take a chance on turning the direction of the American Revolution around.

Nominated by John Adams in 1775 as Commander-in-Chief of the Continental Army, Washington faced a bleak winter after his defeat on Long Island by British troops. From there, his steadily-shrinking army retreated to Manhattan Island. But they could not stay there long. Washington, his back against a wall, faced a fresh attack by the Hessians. Escaping from Manhattan, the little army took refuge on the mainland. There, he fought and lost two more battles. In August 1776, Washington had 28,000 men. Now, in the middle of winter, with men massacred in the attacks in New York and with soldiers daily deserting to return to their families, he had only 6,800 men. As the year drew to a close, the situation looked bleak. The British occupied both Boston and New York.

Colonel John Glover

Colonel Glover evacuates troops from Brooklyn Heights

After the battle of White Plains on October 28th, Washington's demoralized and beaten army slunk back across the North (Hudson) River in order to begin the long trek across New Jersey into Pennsylvania. The Continental Army had suffered terrible losses during 1776. When Washington retreated from New York, he had to abandon forts Washington and Lee, filled with badly-needed munitions and supplies. A large percentage of his troops had been killed or taken prisoner. Winter set in. As the troops retreated into Pennsylvania, taking refuge in Bucks County, their morale sank to an all-time low. Desertion ran high as the weeks inched toward Christmas and soldiers' thoughts turned towards home. Congress had no money to pay them. As both armies retreated into hibernation in their winter quarters, many soldiers wondered if the war for independence could be over.

Washington, gauging the strength and morale of his men, feared that his army would not last through the winter unless he launched a bold attack. His experiences in New York and the Siege of Boston had taught him that his army could not hope to conquer a country controlled by an armed British garrison in every town. Instead, he had to take offensive action, conquering the land, not simply marching through it. According to his intelligence reports, Washington knew that several small outposts near Trenton, New Jersey, under the command of Colonel Rall and Colonel Von Donop would prove the weakest point.

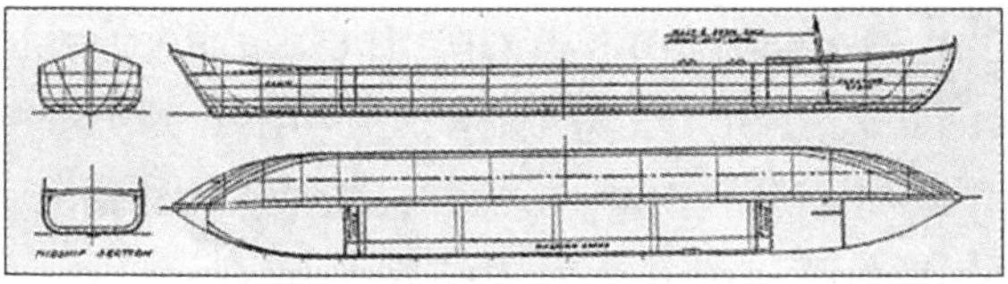

Durham boat used to ferry troops & arms across the Delaware River

Patriots attack Hessian troops at Trenton

Washington had only one problem. Could Washington's soldiers cross the half-frozen Delaware in winter? If one man could do it, he would be Colonel John Glover. His Marblehead Men had participated in the Siege of Boston, creating a fleet of ships known as "Washington's Cruisers." These ships ran military supplies past the British blockade in the Boston Harbor. Glover also covered Washington's troops during the massive evacuation from Brooklyn Heights. In October 1776, he used delay tactics to slow down General William Howe's amphibious landing at Pell's Point on Long Island Sound, buying Washington much-needed time to escape to White Plains and take a stand there. Recognizing his diligence and talents as a seafaring man, Washington asked whether Glover and his Marblehead Men could row the army across in the bad weather. Glover cheerfully urged Washington "not to be troubled about that, as his boys could manage it."

Night fell. About 11 p.m., a terrible snowstorm set in, dumping heavy snow on the ground and causing the temperature to plummet sharply. Chunks of ice formed on the Delaware, delaying the crossing. Washington ordered his men to gather all available boats in the area. Hauling large Durham boats to the water's edge, the Marblehead Men began ferrying the Continental troops across. More than four hundred and five Marblehead Men participated. When Congress declared in 1776 that Black men who served their country at Cambridge could reenlist in the Continental Army, many of them joined Glover's regiment. As Glover watched them straining against the oars with the other sailors, he remembered working side by side with them on his fishing smacks (small fishing boats), living near them in Marblehead, and attending the same church on Sundays together. For Glover, having lived, worked, and prayed with these men, he had no problem fighting beside them.

The snowstorm thickened. The men could see nothing through the swirling white blanket. Meanwhile, on shore, General Henry Knox, Washington's Chief of Artillery, realized that the

Hessians surrender to General Washington

snow would dampen the powder, making it difficult to fire their guns. Recognizing the importance of the artillery to victory, Knox ordered his artillerymen to load eighteen cannons onto the Durham boats.

While the Marblehead Men pushed on steadily through the ice-choked waters, Washington divided his troops into three units. Each man, staring at the dim opposite shore, kept the watchword on his lips: "Victory or Death." That night, the phrase was new to them, inspired by Thomas Paine's recently-published work, "The American Crisis." On the Pennsylvania side, the other Continental commanders prepared to carry out their instructions. Lieutenant John Calwalader, striking out with his Philadelphia Associators from the Bristol Ferry at 4 p.m., would attack or divert Hessian Colonel Von

Donop's men stationed near Mount Holly. While these diversionary tactics kept Von Donop busy, another unit would attack Colonel Rall's detachment stationed alone in Trenton. At the same time, patriot General Ewing had orders to swing across the Delaware at Trenton Ferry with his men from the Bucks County militia. Once across, they would blend into the winter foliage on the south side of the Assupink Creek. From there, they could hold the bridge, cutting off the Hessians' escape route.

Finally, at Trenton, General Washington, accompanied by his "warhorses", Generals Nathanael Greene, Henry Knox, John Sullivan, and Colonel John Glover, intended to appear armed with twenty-four hundred troops, between fifty and seventy-five horses, eighteen cannons, and wagons full of baggage. Battling stinging sleet, giant ice floes jutting out of the water, and severe flooding conditions across the eight hundred-foot-wide river, the Marblehead Men proved that they were worth a dozen other regiments that night.

Ferrying the last Continental soldiers across to McKonkey's Ferry Inn, the Marblehead Men joined the line of cold and tattered patriots for the nine-mile march to Trenton. Glover's men, along with the troops that they ferried across, proved the only Continentals to cross the Delaware that night. Blocked by the freezing sleet, flood conditions, and ice, Calwalader struggled to get his artillery across, but failed without the help of tough, experienced fishermen like the Marbleheaders. Ewing, in turn, simply gave up. Trudging through the snow in the early hours of Christmas Day, the men finally arrived at Trenton at 4 a.m., several hours later, just as dawn began to pale the sky. Realizing that he had lost the cover of darkness, Washington still prepared to launch the attack on the Hessian garrison.

General Washington arrives at Trenton

Grouping the men together, Washington divided his army into opposite camps to begin a two-pronged attack. At 6 a.m., Glover's Marblehead Men and the other Continental soldiers launched themselves at the Hessian outpost. Chaos broke out as Hessian soldiers, sleepy and groggy from celebrating Christmas the night before, ran from the huts straight into the arms of the Continental soldiers. During the next thirty-six hours of fighting, the Marblehead Men rounded up over nine hundred captured Hessian and British soldiers. Washington did not lose a single man and only several were wounded, including young James Monroe and William Washington.

Having shown their steel in fighting as well as ferrying, Glover's men stowed troops, prisoners, captured supplies, and brass cannons in the Durham boats and carried them back across the ice-choked Delaware. After several hours of rowing, every man reached the safety of the opposite shore thanks to the hard work and diligence shown by the Marblehead Men.

The patriot victory at Trenton proved a major turning point in the American Revolution. Not only had George Washington launched an offensive war, solidifying his role as a military leader, but the Christmas Day victory boosted the Continental Army's sagging morale, making it ready to face the trials and victories in the coming year. The diligence demonstrated by Colonel John Glover and the Marblehead Men caused historian George Trevelyan to later observe: "It may be doubted whether so small a number of men ever employed so short a space of time with greater or more lasting results upon the history of the world."

Questions

1. Who were the Marblehead Men?
2. Who was their Colonel?
3. What were the Hessians doing on Christmas Eve?
4. What shape was the American army in? Why were some of Washington's men deserting?
5. What was Washington's daring plan?
6. What was the main obstacle to accomplishing this plan?
7. What quality was Colonel Glover known for?
8. How did weather complicate the undertaking?
9. What was the watchword whispered among the men?
10. Tell of the incredible diligence and fortitude of the Marblehead Men.
11. What effect did this victory have on the course of the War for Independence?
12. Think of some specific ways you can employ diligence to help your family accomplish important goals.

Endurance

DEFINITION

The inward strength to withstand tribulation with determination

MEMORY VERSE

And let us not be weary in well doing: for in due season we shall reap, if we faint not.

Galatians 6:9

Free Land

Gen. Horatio Gates

Saratoga, New York
September 19–October 7, 1777

The heavy fog shrouding the gloomy heights lifted around ten in the morning. On a rugged autumn field belonging to a Loyalist named John Freedman, two great armies faced each other in deadly combat. Fifty-year-old General Horatio Gates, a veteran of the French and Indian War, weighed his options as commander of the Northern Continental Army, against fifty-one-year-old British general and playwright "Gentleman Johnny" Burgoyne's attack.

As the sun dried the dew on the grass, Burgoyne ordered his 8,000 men to advance in three columns. Placing Baron Friedrich Adolf Riedesel on the left, Burgoyne deployed his Hessian troops and the 47th British foot soldiers along the river road. The main artillery, boats, and supplies followed the same route. Meanwhile, General James Inglis Hamilton swung around with his 9th, 20th, and 62nd regiments to attack the high ground. The remainder of the army, under General Simon Fraser, formed the right wing with the elite light infantry and grenadier regiments. Fraser intended to execute a flanking movement, slipping up on the American position. He advanced along the densely-wooded bluffs to the north and west of Bemis Heights.

Meanwhile, Gates deployed his twelve thousand men, assigning his left wing to Colonel Benedict Arnold, while he took command on the right. Next, Gates sent General Benjamin Lincoln with a body of troops to harass the rear of the British army. Gates and Arnold did not get along. Arnold considered "Granny Gates" too timid, preferring an offensive move, while Gates adopted a defensive strategy. Arnold, realizing that the British might try to conduct a flanking movement, begged Gates to let him move his forces from the heights. Once in the woodlands, his country sharpshooters could slip through the trees more easily than the British. Gates preferred to sit tight and wait for Burgoyne to attack. But he agreed to let Morgan's sharpshooters and Henry Dearborn's light infantry advance into the woods.

General Horatio Gates

As they emerged from the trees onto Freeman's field, Morgan's skirmishers spotted British troops with their tall knee-boots advancing towards them. Fraser's men had not yet reached the field, while Hamilton's men still struggled up a ravine through dense forest and over rough terrain. Both sides coiled themselves and prepared for an attack.

The Continental Army had suffered a slow, steady retreat since "Gentleman Johnny" captured Fort Ticonderoga on Lake Champlain in early July. Now, Burgoyne intended to isolate New England by securing the entire upper Hudson Valley. Washington, worried about General William Howe's movements, decided to discover his purpose. His spies informed Washington that Burgoyne had begun to move, while Howe sailed south, not to join Burgoyne, but to capture Philadelphia.

Washington quickly ordered General Israel Putnam's troops and Colonel Daniel Morgan's crack riflemen to join up with Gates' army. At this point, a trapped Burgoyne realized that he needed to entrench himself in easily-defensible quarters for the winter. In order to achieve this, he would either have to retreat to Ticonderoga or advance on Albany. He chose the latter course. Gathering thirty days' rations, Burgoyne crossed the Hudson River during September 13-15, and took up a strong position to the north of Saratoga. As soon as he crossed, however, logistical and supply difficulties began to bog Burgoyne down.

On September 7th, Gates marched north with his army. Arriving ten miles south of Saratoga, he chose Bemis Heights for its defensible high ground. His men set to work like ants, busily building defensive works under the supervision of Polish engineer Thaddeus Kosciusko. Gates knew that the heights overlooked the entire area, and the only road to Albany led through a narrow gap sandwiched between the heights and the Hudson River. Heavily forested bluffs rolled away to the west. These would slow down any advancing army travelling with "Gentleman Johnny's" string of supply wagons.

Burgoyne, meanwhile, felt his way carefully through the hostile countryside. His Native American scouts had abandoned him, leaving him blind as to the American position. Finally, his vanguard arrived at a point just four miles from the American line on September 18th. Several brief skirmishes erupted that same day between American scouting parties and Burgoyne's patrols.

As Arnold's men faced the British in Freedman's field on September 19th, both sides recognized the importance of the American left. Much of the ensuing battle would focus on an attempt to secure the heights. While Fraser's and Arnold's men faced off near the woods, Riedesel's men struggled down a road blocked by trees chopped down by the Americans in an effort to slow their advance. Suddenly, gunfire broke out to the west. Riedesel immediately diverted some of his artillery and sent them ahead down a track towards the sounds of gunfire. Morgan's men, hidden behind the trees, waited as the Redcoats advanced. Aiming carefully, they picked off nearly every British officer in the advance column.

Morgan gave the order to charge. His men catapulted into the center column, not realizing that they faced the bulk of Burgoyne's main army directly behind it. As they pushed back the first company, Fraser's troops ran up and dove into the attack, threatening Morgan's left. His skirmishers scattered back into the woods. James Wilkinson, nudging his horse forward to observe the firing, turned and galloped back to the American camp to secure reinforcements. Fraser's men, colliding with the other British company, opened fire on the flank, accidently killing some of their own men.

The fighting lulled around 1 p.m. in the afternoon. Hamilton deployed his men at the north edge of the field as American reinforcements from the 1st and 3rd New Hampshire, 2nd New York, the 1st Canadian, and Connecticut militia began pouring in from the south. General Enoch Poor's brigade followed hard on their heels. Burgoyne immediately pitched Hamilton's troops into the fight, positioning the 21st on the right, the 20th on the left, and the 62nd in the center. He held the 9th back as a reserve. For the rest of the day, the fighting ebbed between periods of intense combat and sudden lulls. Morgan's men regrouped in the woods, furiously picking off officers and artillerymen crouching behind their cannons and artillery. The Americans' accurate fire allowed the patriots to briefly capture the enemy artillery several times. Each time the British charged, however, the British recaptured their guns. The Americans thrust forward, nearly penetrating the British center at one point, while the Redcoats reformed with difficulty.

At 3 p.m., a hot and nervous Riedesel sent a messenger galloping to Burgoyne for instructions. The man appeared two hours later with orders from "Gentlemen Johnny" to guard the precious supply

General John Burgoyne

wagons. Without supplies, the battle would quickly end in favor of the Americans. At the same time, Burgoyne ordered Riedesel to attack the American right flank with as many men as he could spare. Riedesel decided to take the gamble. Leaving five hundred men to guard the supply wagons, he marched off double-quick with two companies toward the American right. Wading into the fight, the British opened a withering fire on the patriot position. Fraser, maneuvering his troops skillfully, poised to turn the American left flank. If he succeeded, he would roll the entire left wing of the American army up like a carpet and drive straight to the center. A successful flanking movement spelled the end to any conflict.

Battle of Saratoga

Arnold anticipated the move. He appealed to Gates for help. Gates immediately dispatched General

Ebenezer Learned's brigade to the rescue. Before the British could attack, darkness crept among the trees, blotting out the American lines and ending the battle for the night. Licking their light wounds, the patriots moved back through the dark autumn woods and took up their place on the high ground. The British camped on the bloody field that night. During the five-hour battle, they had taken nearly six hundred casualties. Three-quarters of Burgoyne's artillerymen lay dead or wounded. The Americans, by contrast, had lost exactly half as much.

Burgoyne called a council of war. Should he attack the next day? Instead, he decided to delay action until September 21st. His men moved to consolidate their position closer to the American line and collect their dead. Due to a letter from General Henry Clinton in New York City, instructing Burgoyne to attack, instead at Fort Montgomery ten days later, Burgoyne called off the September 21 attack. In no way could Clinton hope to reach Burgoyne, whose food and men were running dangerously low, in time.

When Gates turned in his report on the battle of September 19th, he did not mention Arnold's role at all. Arnold confronted Gates, and the quarrel soon escalated into a shouting match. As a result, Gates relieved Arnold of command and put General Benjamin Lincoln in his place. Meanwhile, American pickets kept running into British patrols, while Morgan's crafty sharpshooters, skilled in backwoods warfare, harassed British troops along the western flank.

As September passed, Burgoyne knew that Clinton would not be coming to help him. Faced with dwindling resources, he had cut his men's food supply, putting them on half rations on September 3rd. At a new council of war, both Riedesel and Fraser encouraged Burgoyne to retreat before it proved too late. Burgoyne refused. He could not retreat—it would be disgraceful. Instead, Burgoyne decided to attack the American left flank with about 2,000 men, more than one-third of his army. By October 7th, Burgoyne faced a rapidly growing force of more than 12,000 American troops. Gates, meanwhile, received daily reports on the British situation from half-starved deserters crossing over to the American lines. In addition to this, Gates had intercepted Clinton's letter responding to Burgoyne's cry for help. As the two armies faced off for battle, Gates knew that Burgoyne could only put 5,000 men into the fight.

As his supply line reached a critical stage, Burgoyne determined to reconnoiter along the left of the American flank instead of retreating. Riedesel and Fraser, at the head of the Advanced Corps, and several companies of light troops and British grenadiers left camp between 10 and 11 a.m. on October 7th in order to probe the left line. They advanced three-quarters of a mile until they reached Barber's Field. Pausing on a rise above Mill Brook, the redcoats scanned the patriot lines. The Hessians deployed to the center, while eight British cannons rolled into position.

The field gave the artillery range to play, but the

Patriots charge British defenses

British flanks came treacherously close to the dark woods surrounding them. In camp, Gates listened as American scouts hurried in with news that Burgoyne had gone on the move. Immediately, Gates ordered Morgan's riflemen to deploy to the far left, while he placed Poor's men on the right and sent Learned's regulars and militia to the center. Meanwhile, a force of 1,200 New York militiamen under General Abraham Ten Broeck remained in reserve behind Learned's line.

The battle opened between 2:00 and 2:30 p.m. when British grenadiers fired on General Enoch Poor's men. The Americans held their fire as British bullets bounced off the uneven terrain. When British aim proved ineffective, Major Acland gathered his British grenadiers for a desperate bayonet charge. The patriots waited until the Redcoats came close enough to see the whites of their eyes and then opened fire at close range. Morgan's sharpshooters, hiding among the trees, took out Major Acland. The British officer fell, shot through both legs, as the sharpshooters mowed his men down. Turning, the survivors fled with Poor's men at their heels. On the way, the Americans scooped up Acland as a prisoner and captured the royal artillery.

Meanwhile, on the American left, things went downhill for Burgoyne's men. Morgan's somewhat outnumbered sharpshooters advanced, pushing aside a small Canadian contingent and a group of Native Americans to engage with Fraser's British regulars. Together with Enoch Poor's men, Morgan managed to block and destroy a number of British endeavors to advance west. Suddenly, Fraser fell, and British morale crumpled. Weak with hunger from half rations and badly outnumbered, the British began a messy retreat towards their entrenchments. Nearby, "Gentleman Johnny" almost died when one of Morgan's sharpshooters aimed at him and pulled the trigger. Three bullets ripped into his horse, hat, and waistcoat. The first part of the battle had lasted only one hour. Burgoyne had lost almost four hundred men. He had also lost most of his grenadiers, as well as six of the ten valuable field pieces on the battlefield.

Just then, Arnold, furious at his removal from command, and possibly drunk, galloped out onto the battlefield. Worried, Gates dispatched Major Armstrong to follow Arnold and order him to return. Armstrong set out, but did not catch up with Arnold until darkness fell. Meanwhile, the British retreated towards their camp and barricaded themselves in the closer of two redoubts stationed on either side. One, under a commander named Breymann, contained three hundred men. The other, led by Colonel Balcarres, stood further to the west. Arnold set off after the Redcoats, heading the attack by Poor's men on the Balcarres fortification. As the patriots attacked the redoubt, furious fighting broke out.

The British, however, defended their position savagely, causing the American advance to grind to a halt. At that moment, Arnold rushed forward, galloping between the lines. He burst through, unhurt, to lead Learned's men in a charge on the Breymann redoubt. The Americans burst over the defenses, killing the commander Breymann. A final volley pierced Arnold's leg and struck his horse. The animal plunged and fell, rolling over on Arnold's leg and breaking the bone. Darkness set in as Major Armstrong finally caught up, panting. Finding Arnold pinned under his horse, the Major had Arnold carried back to headquarters in a litter. The sun went down behind the high ground, silhouetting the captured Breymann redoubt. The American charge had exposed the British camp. Near sundown, a contingent of Hessians attempted to recapture the position. In the darkness, an untrustworthy guide led them over the rough terrain and straight into the American lines. The final counterattack by the Hessians ended in their capture.

Between the battles at Freedman's Farm and Bemis Heights, "Gentleman Johnny" lost one thousand soldiers, leaving him outnumbered three to one. Gates, in contrast, suffered about five hundred dead and wounded. A large number of British officers lay dead, while the Americans had managed to pierce Burgoyne's forward line. Desperate, with his men on half rations, Burgoyne lit bonfires in front of the few forward positions he had left. Then the British general gathered his remaining men and pulled back under cover of night. Retreating in the darkness, "Gentleman Johnny" managed to slip into the same defensible positions that he had occupied on September 16th to the north of the village of Saratoga.

But "Gentleman Johnny's" luck had run out. The American forces had swelled to include Lincoln's returning detachment, while militiamen, ammunition, and supplies constantly poured to the front. By October 13th, almost 20,000 American troops surrounded Burgoyne at Saratoga. On October 14th, Burgoyne bowed to fate and opened negotiations to surrender. Three days later, the most fashionable man in the British army surrendered his entire force, consisting of 5,000 British and Hessian troops—the largest surrender of British forces in the Revolutionary War to date. Burgoyne met with Gates to sign the Convention of Saratoga, while the remnants of the British expedition left at Fort Ticonderoga straggled back to Quebec. The Continental Congress kept the nearly 6,000-man army as prisoners at high expense until the war ended. The survivors returned to Britain, after vowing never to fight in the American colonies again.

Flush with victory, Gates wanted to follow up the battle by invading Quebec. Washington, however, rejected the idea. Following the battles at Saratoga, Congress restored Gates to a senior command in the Department of the South. Congress also presented Gates with a gold medal to commemorate his triumph. Gates is depicted in the center of John Trumbull's famous painting: *Surrender of General Burgoyne.*

Today, it hangs in the U.S. Capitol Rotunda in Washington, D.C. Gates had won the greatest American victory up to that point. He would never reach such heights again, suffering a catastrophic defeat at Camden in 1780. Congress also declared a national day "for solemn Thanksgiving and praise" on December 18, 1777. It would become the United

States' first official observance of a holiday by that name.

The Surrender of General Burgoyne

The most significant outcome of Saratoga was that it proved a turning point in the war. It prompted King Louis XVI of France to negotiate with American ambassador Benjamin Franklin to join forces with the colonies in a Franco-American alliance. When the French entered the war on the American side, the Revolution went from a local to a global stage. As a result of Saratoga and French support, the British had to redirect supplies used to fight the war in North America to battlegrounds in Europe and the West Indies.

Gates and his men demonstrated endurance, proving to the British that the Americans could face them in stand-up combat with courage, obstinacy, and fortitude. They had fought for a free land. Having gained one of the greatest victories up to that point, the patriots had hope that dream could finally come true.

...a Reverence for our great Creator, Principles of Humanity, and the Dictates of Common Sense, must convince all those who reflect upon the Subject, that Government was instituted to promote the Welfare of Mankind, and ought to be administered for the Attainment of that End....

—From the version of the "Declaration of the Causes and Necessity for Taking Up Arms", July 6, 1775; Continental Congress

Questions

1. How old was General Horatio Gates?
2. How many men did Burgoyne have? How many did Gates have?
3. What did Burgoyne decide to do when Israel Putnam's and Daniel Morgan's men joined up with Gates' army?
4. Where did Gates choose to build his defensive works?
5. How many casualties did the British suffer during the five-hour battle?
6. What was Burgoyne's next move?
7. How did Arnold's leg get broken?
8. How many troops surrounded Burgoyne at Saratoga?
9. What was the most significant outcome of the Battle of Saratoga?
10. How did General Gates and his men demonstrate endurance?
11. Think of a situation in your life where you could apply endurance.

Wisdom

DEFINITION

Learning to see life from
God's point of view

MEMORY VERSE

If any of you lack wisdom, let him
ask of God, that giveth to all men l
iberally, and upbraideth not;
and it shall be given him.

James 1:5

Starving Winter

Gen. George Washington

Valley Forge, Pennsylvania

December 1777

As the first snow fell, covering White Marsh, General George Washington began pulling his troops back after their last fight with the British at Edge Hill. With winter hovering on the verge of woods and streams, making the edges of rivers crackle with ice, the Commander-in-Chief of the Continental Army began hunting for a winter camp. Twenty-five miles northwest of Pennsylvania, he came upon an iron forge located on Valley Creek. He had found a spot close enough to keep the

Soldiers building cabins at Valley Forge

Redcoats from raiding and harassing the heart of Pennsylvania. At the same time, the army could bunk down for the winter at a distance that diminished the possibility of a surprise attack.

On December 19th, just days before Christmas, 12,000 exhausted Continental soldiers stumbled into the camp at Valley Forge. High mountains surrounded them on all sides. Flanked on one side by Mount Joy and on the other by Mount Misery, the men could see the steel-grey strip of the Schuylkill River to the north, that together with the mountains, fenced them in like a triangle. When the men arrived, worn out from their long march, they saw only an empty space without fire or shelter. Only about a third of the soldiers had shoes, and blood stained the snow into the camp. The wind picked up, cutting their faces with a warning taste of winter.

General Washington reviewing the troops at Valley Forge

Work on the huts began immediately. Within three days, they had the first hut up, but the others took longer. With only one axe between them, the men had to trudge several miles through the snow to chop down timber and drag it back to camp. After they cut down eighty logs, the heavy work of lifting and constructing the larger cabin began. It took the half-starved men a week to complete it. Meanwhile, officers planned out lines of defense and established quarters for the brigades. Six weeks later, the men were under cover. But serious supply shortages continued to threaten the army.

Washington praying at Valley Forge

As the long Pennsylvania winter set in, tattered Continental soldiers huddled around meager fires, trying to keep warm. Outside, shallow snow covered the ground. Snow fell rarely, but it continually melted and froze again, soaking through the soldiers' foot-wrappings to fester against sore and irritated flesh. Shoes wore out and could not be replaced. Their frozen feet, wrapped in rags, left bloody prints in the snow. Few men possessed a blanket. Supplies of meat and bread dwindled. Some of the men scraped together "fire cake," a paste made from flour mixed with water. Wounded soldiers died from severe exposure, while hunger and disease rendered another 4,000 men incapacitated for duty. Typhoid, dysentery, jaundice, and pneumonia stalked the camp. Hundreds of horses starved where they stood or wandered away among the trees to die.

At army headquarters, George Washington admitted that he did not know how they could survive. "Unless some great and capital change suddenly takes place," he wrote, "... this Army must inevitably ... starve, dissolve, or disperse, in order to obtain subsistence in the best manner they can."

As he left the small grey stone house that served as his headquarters, Washington moved past small groups of soldiers drilling during the short winter afternoon. The harsh Prussian voice of Baron Friedrich von Steuben rang through the air.

Despite the cold, damp wind, Washington saw the men's backs straighten, their heads come erect and their bloody feet determinedly stamp the frozen ground. Putting daily drill into their routine had given the hungry soldiers a new sense of morale. Sometimes it seemed as if the army was surviving on morale alone.

On a day of Thanksgiving issued by Congress, each soldier's meal consisted of just half a cup of rice and one tablespoonful of vinegar. By Christmas, Washington knew that the army could not exist like this. They needed help to preserve the cause of freedom.

A twenty-six-year-old Quaker named Isaac Potts was riding down a wooded slope towards the snow-sprinkled plain near Washington's headquarters. At the height of the revolution, Potts found himself in a strange position as both a pacifist and a Tory. Believing that war and rebellion against authority was a sin, Potts believed that the colonists would ultimately fail in their struggle for independence. Now, deep in Montgomery County, the young Quaker plodded through the snow close by the huddled encampment of the American Army. Suddenly, he heard a pleading voice rise and fall on the cold air. He stopped his horse, craning his neck to stare among the trees. Then he tied his horse to a sapling and dismounted. Quietly pushing through the grey, dead underbrush near the creek, Potts suddenly emerged into a clearing surrounded by giant, dark oaks.

There before him he saw George Washington kneeling alone in the snow. His sword hung at his side. His cocked hat lay beside him on the ground. Tears streamed down his face. He prayed aloud, to the God of victories, to bless and protect his army. The cause of freedom did not depend on the starving, ragged men holding out in Valley Forge, but on a power higher than any of them imagined. Alone, pushed back by British victories and supported by

Isaac Potts house used by Washington as his headquarters

a Congress that could not feed its own soldiers, the army staggered on the brink of extinction. Dozens of men and officers slipped away into the woods each day, consumed by gnawing hunger, fear of disease, and anxiety for their families struggling to survive on small farms harassed by British troops. Washington knew how hard the remaining men tried to keep on, how they drilled bravely in their bloody feet while their rags flapped in the wind. He had walked through the camp and seen wounded men frozen to death on the ground. Others, their legs turned black from frostbite, had to have feet and legs amputated. They needed supplies, but most of all they needed hope—an assurance that they would live through the winter and that all their sacrifices would not have been for nothing. The prayer went on and on, the air reverberating with the emotion in that deep, anguished voice.

Isaac Potts rode home in a kind of daze. He burst into tears as he threw open the door to the parlor and called out to his wife.

"Sarah, my dear Sarah! All's well! All's well! George Washington will yet prevail."

His wife stared at him. "What's the matter, Isaac?" she demanded. "Thee seems moved."

The Quaker could not contain himself. "Well, if I seem moved, 'tis no more than what I really am. I have this day seen what I never expected. Thee knows that I always thought that the sword and the gospel were utterly inconsistent; and that no man could be a soldier and a Christian at the same time. But George Washington has this day convinced me of my mistake."

The story tumbled from him: the bitter cold, the lonely place, and the sight of the commander of the army on his knees in prayer. "If there is anyone on this earth whom the Lord will listen to, it is George Washington," he told Sarah.

He paused, remembering the calm, almost unearthly look he had seen on Washington's face that day in the woods. Then he spoke. "If George Washington be not a man of God, I am greatly deceived—and still more shall I be deceived, if God do not, through him, work out a great salvation for America."

Washington's prayers were soon answered. Going out one foggy morning, a number of soldiers saw that the Schuylkill River no longer wore its placid winter sheath of ice. Instead, the water seemed to be boiling and tossing. Going closer, the men saw that thousands of shad were struggling to swim upstream. Ordinarily, no fish would begin to migrate this early without signs of spring. But the miracle had happened. Grabbing pitchforks and shovels, the soldiers lunged into the river. Wading in among the ice floes, they began tossing the fish up onto the bank. Then "Light-horse" Harry Lee and his soldiers rode their horses straight into the water to corral the shad and keep them from darting away. Working together, the men dragged in great amounts of fish. That day, there was suddenly an abundance of food for the army.

When the Continental Army broke camp and left Valley Forge on June 19, 1778, after six months of hardship, they pursued the British who headed towards New York. George Washington demonstrated such great wisdom in placing his faith and trust in the Supreme Judge of heaven and earth for guidance and direction in the weighty responsibility placed upon him as Commander-in-Chief. Today we are the beneficiaries of the blessings of Washington's God-given wisdom.

If George Washington be not a man of God, I am greatly deceived—and still more shall I be deceived, if God do not, through him, work out a great salvation for America.

—Isaac Potts

Questions

1. Why did General Washington choose Valley Forge as the camp to spend the winter?
2. How many soldiers arrived there on December 19th?
3. Had Congress made provisions for the troops at Valley Forge?
4. How long did it take the men to get shelters built?
5. What condition were the soldier's clothes and shoes in?
6. What did the men often have to eat?
7. What diseases did they face?
8. What did the soldiers have to eat on Thanksgiving Day?
9. Tell about the experience Issac Potts, the Tory, had.
10. What did George Washington pray?
11. How was Potts affected by hearing the prayer? What did he proclaim to his wife?
12. How were Washington's prayers answered?
13. What is wisdom? How did General Washington demonstrate wisdom? What was the result?

Selected Bibliography

Adams, John, and L. H. Butterfield. *Diary and Autobiography of John Adams, Vol. II.* Cambridge: Harvard University Press, 1962.

Aldridge, Alfred O. *Benjamin Franklin and Nature's God.* Durham, N.C.: Duke University Press, 1967.

Allison, Robert. *The Boston Massacre.* Beverly, MA: Applewood Books, 2006.

Amler, Jane Frances. *Haym Solomon: Patriot Banker of the American Revolution.* Powerkids Press, 2004.

Ammon, Richard. *Valley Forge.* Holiday House, 2006.

Anderson, Fred. *Crucible of War: The Seven Years' War and the Fate of Empire in British North America: 1754-1766.* New York: Alfred A. Knopf, 2000.

Archer, Richard. *As if an Enemy's Country: the British Occupation of Boston and the Origins of Revolution.* Oxford, New York: Oxford University Press, 2010.

Barton, Charles D. *The Bulletproof George Washington.* Wallbuilders Press, 1990.

Barton, David. *The Jefferson Lies.* Thomas Nelson, 2012. (This is an excellent book and we highly recommend it. It is thoroughly documented and also dispels other myths about Jefferson so prevalently believed today.)

Beliles, Mark A. and Stephen K. McDowell. *America's Providential History.* Charlottesville, Virginia: Providence Foundation, 1989.

Bessette, Joseph M. and John J. Pitney, Jr. *American Government and Politics: Deliberation, Democracy and Citizenship.* Boston: Wadsworth Cengage Learning, 2011.

Billias, George Athan. *General John Glover and his Marblehead Mariners.* New York: Holt, Rinehart & Winston, 1960.

Bobrick, Benson. *Angel in the Whirlwind: The Triumph of the American Revolution.* New York: Simon & Schuster, 2011.

Bodie, Idella. *The Man Who Loved the Flag.* Heroes and Heroines of the American Revolution. 2008.

Bowdoin, James, Samuel Adams, et al. *A Short Narrative of the Horrid Massacre.* London: W. Bingley, 1770.

Bowen, Catherine Drinker. *Miracle at Philadelphia: The Story of the Constitutional Convention: May to September 1787.* New York: Book-of-the-Month Club, Inc., 1986.

Boyd, Julian P. and Gerard W. Gawalt. *The Declaration of Independence: The Evolution of the Text.* University Press of New England, 1999.

Brady, Patricia. *Martha Washington: An American Life.* New York: Viking Press, 2005.

Brandt, Clare. *The Man in the Mirror: A Life of Benedict Arnold.* New York: Random House, 1994.

Brookhiser, Richard. *James Madison.* Basic Books, 2011.

Brooks, Victor. *The Boston Campaign.* Conshohocken, PA: Combined Publishing, 1999.

Buchanan, John. *The Road to Valley Forge: How Washington Built the Army that Won the Revolution.* Wiley: 2004.

Burnett, Edward Cody. *The Continental Congress.* New York: Norton, 1941.

Burnham, Norman Hammond. *The Battle of Groton Heights: A Story of the Storming of Fort Griswold and the Burning of New London, on the Sixth of September, 1781.* Kessinger Publishing, 2006.

Carbone, Gerald M. *Nathanael Greene: A Biography of the American Revolution.* New York: Palgrave Macmillan, 2010.

Carstens, Kenneth C. and Nancy Son Carstens, eds. *The Life of George Rogers Clark, 1752-1818: Triumphs and Tragedies.* Westport, Connecticut: Praeger, 2004.

Cheney, Lynne. *When Washington Crossed the Delaware: A Wintertime Story for Young Patriots.* New York: Simon & Schuster, 2012.

Chernow, Ron. *Washington: A Life.* New York: Penguin Press, 2010.

Clary, David A. *George Washington's First War: His Early Military Adventures.* New York: Simon & Schuster, 2011.

Coffin, Charles L. *The Boys of '76.* Weiner Media, 2009.

Collier, Christopher. *Decision in Philadelphia: The Constitutional Convention of 1787.* New York: Ballantine Books, 2007.

Collins, Kathleen. *Marquis de Lafayette: French Hero of the American Revolution.* Rosen Central, 2004.

Connecticut Society of the Sons of the American Revolution. *King George's Head.* Sons of the American Revolution, Winter 1998.

Cooley, Timothy Mather. *Sketches of the Life and Character of the Reverend Samuel Haynes, A.M., for Many Years Pastor of a Church in Rutland, Vermont, and Late in Granville, New York.* New York: Negro Universities Press, 1969.

Copp, John J. *The Battle of Groton Heights: The Massacre of Fort Griswold; and the Burning of New London.* Groton Heights Centennial Committee, 1879.

Crocker, Thomas E. *Braddock's March: How the Man Sent to Seize a Continent Changed American History.* Westholme Publishing, 2011.

Crofut, W. A. and John M. Morris. *The Military and Civil History of Connecticut during the War of 1861-65.* Ledyard Bill, 1868.

Dameron, J. David. *Kings Mountain: The Defeat of the Loyalists, October 7, 1780.* Cambridge, Massachusetts: DaCapo Press, 2003.

Davis, Burke. *Black Heroes of the American Revolution.* Sandpiper, 1992.

Dawson, Thomas Fulton. *Life and Character of Edward Oliver Wolcott, Late a Senator of the United States From the State of Colorado.* Forgotten Books, 2012.

Derleth, August. *Vincennes: Portal to the West.* Englewood Cliffs, New Jersey: Prentice-Hall, 1968.

Dorson, Richard M., *Patriots of the American Revolution: True Accounts by Great Americans from Ethan Allen to George Rogers Clark.* New York: Gramercy Books, 1953.

Driver, Carl S. *John Sevier: Pioneer of the Old Southwest.* Chapel Hill: University of North Carolina Press, 1932.

Dunkerly, Robert M. *The Battle of King's Mountain: Eyewitness Accounts.* The History Press, 2007.

Field, Joseph E. *"Worthy Partner": The Papers of Martha Washington*. Praeger Press, 1994.

Finger, John R. *Tennessee Frontiers: Three Regions in Transition.* Indiana University Press, 2001.

Fischer, David Hackett. *Paul Revere's Ride.* New York: Oxford University Press, 1994.

—. *Washington's Crossing.* Oxford University Press, 2006.

Fleming, Thomas. *Washington's Secret War: The Hidden History of Valley Forge.* Harper Perennial, 2006.

Flexner, James Thomas. *The Traitor and the Spy: Benedict Arnold and John Andre.* New York: Little, Brown & Company, 1975.

Foreman, Samuel A. *Dr. Joseph Warren: The Boston Tea Party, Bunker Hill, and the Birth of American Liberty.* New York: Pelican Publishing, 2011.

Freedman, Russell. *Washington at Valley Forge.* Holiday House, 2008.

Frothingham, Richard. *The Life and Times of Joseph Warren.* Applewood Books, 2009.

Fritz, Jean. *Why Not Lafayette?* New York: Puffin, 2001.

Garrison, Webb. *White House Ladies: Fascinating Tales and Colorful Curiosities.* Tennessee: Thomas Nelson Press, 1996.

Gingrich, Newt. *Valley Forge.* St. Martin's Griffin, 2011.

Golway, Terry. *Washington's General: Nathanael Greene and the Triumph of the American Revolution.* New York: Holt, 2005.

Goodrich, Charles A. *Lives of the Signers to the Declaration of Independence.* New York: Thomas Mather, 1832.

Gordon, William. *The History of the Rise, Progress, and Establishment, of the Independence of the United States of America.* Berkeley: University of California Collection, 1788.

Greene, George W. *The Life of Nathanael Greene, Major-General in the Army of the Revolution.* 3 vols. Freeport, NY: Books for Libraries Press, 1972.

Hall, Verna M. *The Christian History of the Constitution of the United States of America.* San Francisco: Foundation for American Christian Education, 1983.

Hanna, Willard A. *The Berkshire–Litchfield Legacy.* C. E. Tuttle and Company, 1984.

Harrison, Lowell H. *George Rogers Clark and the War in the West.* Lexington, Kentucky: University of Kentucky Press, 2001.

Hatch, Robert McConnell. *Major John Andre: A Gallant in Spy's Clothing.* New York: Houghton Mifflin, 1986.

Haugen, Brenda. *Martha Washington: First Lady of the United States.* Compass Point Books, 2005.

Haw, James. "'Every Thing Here Depends upon Opinion': Nathanael Greene and Public Support in the Southern Campaigns of the American Revolution." *South Carolina Historical Magazine,* 109 (July 2008): 212-31.

Heinemann, Ronald L., John G. Kolp, Anthony S. Parent, Jr., and William G. Shade. *Old Dominion, New Commonwealth: A History of Virginia, 1607-2007.* University of Virginia Press, 2007.

Hibbert, Christopher. *Redcoats and Rebels: The War for America 1770-1781.* Grafton Books, 1990.

Hobson, Charles F. and Robert A. Rutlands, eds. *The Papers of James Madison: Volume 12, 2 March 1789-20 January 1790.* Charlottesville: University Press of Virginia, 1979.

Hogeland, William. *Declaration: The Nine Tumultuous Weeks When America Became Independent, May 1–July 4, 1776.* New York: Simon & Schuster, 2010.

Hutchinson, Francis. *A Fair Account of the Late Unhappy Disturbance at Boston.* London: B. White, 1770.

Isaacson, Walter. *Benjamin Franklin: An American Life.* New York: Simon & Schuster, 2004.

Jefferson, Thomas. *Jefferson's "Bible"; The Life and Morals of Jesus of Nazareth XV-XVI.* ed. Judd Patton (Grove City): American Book Distributors, 1996.

Jefferson, Thomas. *The Writings of Thomas Jefferson, Vol. 9.* ed. Paul Leicester Ford. New York: G.P. Putnam's Sons, 1899.

Johnson, Clifton (1915). *The Picturesque Hudson.* MacMillan. Retrieved 2009-07-08.

Jones, Charles Colcock. *Sergeant William Jasper.* Kessinger Publishing, 2010

Kaplan, Sidney, and Emma Nogrady Kaplan. *The Black Presence in the Era of the American Revolution.* Amherst, Massachusetts: The University of Massachusetts Press, 1989.

Ketcham, Ralph Louis. *James Madison: A Biography.* Charlottesville, VA: University of Virginia Press, 1971.

Ketchum, Richard M. *Saratoga: Turning Point of America's Revolutionary War.* New York: Henry Holt, 1997.

Kopperman, Paul. *Braddock at the Monongahela.* Pittsburgh, PA: University of Pittsburgh Press, 1977.

Krensky, Stephen. *DK Biography: Benjamin Franklin.* DK Children, 2007.

Labunski, Richard. *James Madison and the Struggle for the Bill of Rights.* New York, NY: Oxford University Press, 2006.

Lane, Jason. *General and Madame de Lafayette: Partners in Liberty's Cause in the American and French Revolutions.* Taylor Trade Publishing, 2003.

Lindenmeyer, Otto. *Black & Brave: The Black Soldier in America.* New York, 1970.

Loane, Nancy K. *Following the Drum: Women at the Valley Forge Encampment.* Potomac Books, Inc., 2009.

Lockhart, Paul Douglas. *The Drillmaster of Valley Forge: the Baron de Von Steuben and the Making of the American Army.* New York: Harper Collins, 2008.

Lodge, Henry Cabot and Theodore Roosevelt. *Hero Tales from American History,* George Grant, ed. White Hall, West Virginia: Tolle Lege Press, 2012.

Luzader, John F. *Saratoga: A Military History of the Decisive Campaign of the American Revolution.* New York: Savas Beatie, 2010.

Maier, Pauline. *American Scripture: Making the Declaration of Independence.* New York: Knopf, 1997.

Marshall, Peter and David Manuel. *The Light and the Glory.* Revell, 1977.

Martin, James Kirby. *Benedict Arnold, Revolutionary War Hero: An American Warrior Reconsidered.* New York: New York University Press, 1997.

Massachusetts Historical Society. *Henry Knox Diary, 20 November 1775 to 13 January 1776.*

Massey, Gregory D. *General Nathanael Greene and the American Revolution in the South.* University of South Carolina Press, 2012.

McClung, Robert. *Young George Washington and the French and Indian War, 1753-1758.* Linnet Books, 2002.

McCrady, Edward. *The History of South Carolina in the Revolution, 1775-1780.* New York: Macmillan, 1901.

McCullough, David. *1776.* New York: Simon & Schuster, 2005.

Messick, Hank. *King's Mountain: The Epic of the Blue Ridge "Mountain Men" in the American Revolution.* New York: Little & Brown, 1976.

Middlekauff, Robert. *The Glorious Cause: The American Revolution, 1763-1789.* New York and Oxford: Oxford University Press, 2007.

Milgrim, Shirley Gorson. *Haym Salomon: Liberty's Son.* The Jewish Publication Society, 1979.

Mintz, Max M. *The Generals of Saratoga: John Burgoyne and Horatio Gates.* New Haven, Connecticut: Yale University Press, 1990.

Morrissey, Brendan. *Saratoga 1777: Turning Point of a Revolution.* Oxford: Osprey Publishing, 2000.

Morrill, Dan. *Southern Campaigns of the American Revolution.* Nautical & Aviation Publishing, 1993.

National Archives Education Staff. *The Constitution: Evolution of a Government.* Santa Barbara: ABC-CLIO, Inc., 2001.

Pancake, John. *This Destructive War.* University of Alabama Press, 1985.

Payan, Gregory. *Marquis de Lafayette: French Hero of the American Revolution.* The Rosen Publishing Group, 2002.

Peacock, Louise. *Crossing the Delaware: A History in Many Voices.* Aladdin, 2007.

Peters, Madison C. *Haym Salomon: The Financier of the Revolution.* University Press of the Pacific, 2005.

Puls, Mark. *Henry Knox: Visionary General of the American Revolution.* New York: Palgrave, 2010.

Randall, Henry Stephens. *The Life of Thomas Jefferson,* Vol. 3. New York: Derby & Jackson, 1858.

Randall, William Sterne. *Benedict Arnold: Patriot and Traitor.* Dorset Press, 2001.

Randall, Williard Sterne. *Ethan Allen: His Life and Times.* New York: W. W. Norton, 2011.

Reit, Seymour. *Guns for General Washington: A Story of the American Revolution.* Sandpiper, 2001.

Rosen, Gary. *American Compact: James Madison and the Problem of Founding.* Lawrence, Kansas: University Press of Kansas, 1999.

Russell, Charles Edward. *Haym Solomon and the Revolution.* Ayer Company Publishers, 1930.

Rutland, Robert Allen. *James Madison: The Founding Father.* Columbia, MO: University of Missouri Press, 1987.

Saillant, John. *Black Puritan, Black Republican: The Life and Thought of Lemuel Haynes, 1753-1833.* New York: Oxford University Press, 2003.

Savas, Theodore P., and Dameron, J. David. *A Guide to the Battles of the American Revolution.* Savas Beatie, 2005.

Scheer, George F. and Hugh F. Rankin, *Rebels and Redcoats.* New York: The World Publishing Company, 1957.

Schwartz, Laurens R. *Jews and the American Revolution: Haym Solomon and Others,* Jefferson, North Carolina: McFarland & Co., 1987.

Scollay, Mercy to Elijah Dix. "I Wear a Face Foreign to the Feelings of My Heart" (Boston: April 26, 1776). *Mercy Scollay Papers, 1775-1824.* Cambridge Historical Society, Cambridge, Massachusetts.

Silverman, Jerry. *Of Thee I Sing.* Citadel Press, 2002.

Silvey, Anita. *Henry Knox: Bookseller, Soldier, Patriot.* Clarion Books, 2010.

Simpson, Andrew. "In St. Patrick's Shadow: The Peculiar Holiday of Evacuation Day," *The Bostonian Society News* (2004, Issue 1).

Steele, William O. *John Sevier: Pioneer Boy. The Childhood of Famous Americans Series.* Indianapolis: Bobbs-Merrill, 1953.

Stewart, David O. *The Summer of 1787: The Men Who Invented the Constitution.* New York: Simon & Schuster, 2008.

Sumner Letter, "Boston 1775," accessed on 02/08/2013.

Tonsetic, Robert. *1781: The Decisive Year of the Revolutionary War.* Casemate, 2011.

Uhlar, Janet. *Liberty's Martyr: The Story of Dr. Joseph Warren.* Dog Ear Publishing, 2009.

Unger, Harlow Giles. *Lafayette.* Hoboken, New Jersey: John Wiley & Sons, 2002.

Vile, John R. *The Constitutional Convention of 1787: A Comprehensive Encyclopedia of America's Founding.* 2 Vols. ABC-CLIO: 2005.

Walett, Francis. "James Bowdoin, Patriot Propagandist." *The New England Quarterly:* 23:3 (September 1950).

Ware, Susan. *Forgotten Heroes: Inspiring American Portraits from Our Leading Historians.* Portland, Oregon: Simon & Schuster, 2000.

Warren, Joseph. *The Suffolk Resolves,* September 9, 1774.

Washington, George to Martha Washington, "My Dearest Life and Love," June 24, 1776.

Washington, George to William Gordon. "8 July 1788." *Writings,* 27: 49-52.

Wheeler, Richard "Little Bear." *God's Mighty Hand: Providential Occurrences in World History,* Bulverde, Texas: Mantle Ministries Press.

Wheeler, William Bruce, Susan Becker, and Lorri Glover. *Discovering the American Past: A Look at the Evidence: To 1877.* Belmont, CA: Cengage Learning, 2011.

White, Alain C. *The History of the Town of Litchfield, Connecticut, 1720-1920.* Litchfield, Connecticut: Enquirer Print, 1920.

White, Richard. *Jordan Freeman Was My Friend.* Xlibris Corps, 2003. (Historical Fiction)

Wilson, Barry K. *Benedict Arnold: A Traitor in Our Midst.* McGill Queens Press, 2001.

York, Neil Longley. *The Boston Massacre: A History with Documents.* New York: Taylor & Francis, 2010.

Websites and Other Media

Brennan, Daniel. "Did James Madison suffer a nervous collapse due to the intensity of his studies?" Mudd Manuscript Library Blog, January 2008, Princeton University Archives and Public Policy Papers Collection, Princeton University.

Fowler, William M. "Glover, John." *American National Biography Online,* www.anb.org/ February 2000.

Garden, Alexander. *"Sergeant Jasper, 2nd Regiment." Anecdotes of the Revolutionary War in America. 1822.* http://books.google.com/books?id=WJ98ynQ-W-AC&pg=PA90

"Henry Knox and the 'Noble Train of Artillery' " on the *Fort Ticonderoga National Historic Landmark* http://www.fort-ticonderoga.org/history/bibliographies/henry_knox.htm

"Heralds of a Liberal Faith," Volumes I-IV. http://harvardsquarelibrary.org/Heralds/Jonathan-Mayhew.php

Sevier, William Jay, and Lance Sevier. "The Life of John Sevier Time Line, Including Family Origins & World Events, 1506 -1815." http://www.johnsevier.com/jstime.html

"Saratoga National Historical Park." National Park Service. http://www.nps.gov/sara/.

(Documentary DVD) *Von Steuben's Continentals: The First American Army* (Actor: John D. Pagano, Lionheart Filmworks, 2007).

Photo credits

Attentiveness

Portrait of Samuel Fraunces: Public Domain. http://en.wikipedia.org/wiki/File:Samuel_Fraunces_Portrait_circa_1770-85_from_Fraunces_Tavern.jpg

Fraunces' Tavern: New York Public Library. http://digitalgallery.nypl.org/nypldigital/dgkeysearchdetail.cfm?strucID=691818&imageID=804911&k=0&print=small

Washington's farewell to officers / H.A. Ogden. Library of Congress. https://www.loc.gov/resource/pga.07801/

Diligence

Drawing of Col. Glover: Public Domain. http://en.wikipedia.org/wiki/File:Appletons%27_Glover_John.jpg

Passage of the Delaware: Public Domain. http://en.wikipedia.org/wiki/File:1819_Passage_OfThe_Delaware_byThomasSully_MFABoston.jpeg

Durham boats: http://www.living-in-the-past.com/waterways.html

Battle of Trenton (2): Public Domain. http://ushistory-images.com/battle-of-trenton.shtm

Glover at Brooklyn Heights: http://www.revolutionary-wararchives.org/glover.html

Endurance

General Horatio Gates Portrait: Public Domain. http://en.wikipedia.org/wiki/File:HoratioGatesByStuart_crop.jpg

General John Burgoyne portrait: Public Domain. http://en.wikipedia.org/wiki/File:BurgoyneByReynolds.jpg

Surrender of General Burgoyne: Public Domain. http://en.wikipedia.org/wiki/File:Surrender_of_General_Burgoyne.jpg

Battle of Saratoga: Public Domain. http://ushistoryimages.com/battle-of-saratoga.shtm

Battle of Freeman's Farm: http://61354085.nhd.weebly.com/uploads/1/6/3/7/16370714/203607_orig.jpg?247

Honesty

John Hart Portrait: illustration by Linda J. Linder, *For You They Signed,* Marilyn Boyer, Rustburg, VA, The Learning Parent, 2008

Sourland Mountains: http://en.wikipedia.org/wiki/File:SourlandBoulderField.jpg

Perseverance

Ox train: http://www.tumblr.com/tagged/fort%20ticonderoga?page=19, painting by Tom Lovell

Gen. Henry Knox Portrait: Public Domain. http://en.wikipedia.org/wiki/File:Henry_Knox_by_Peale.jpg, painting by Charles Wilson Peale

Knox-Ticonderoga: Public Domain. http://ushistoryimages.com/fort-ticonderoga.shtm

Knox returning to camp: Public Domain. http://en.wikipedia.org/wiki/File:Henry_Knox_entering_camp_with_artillery_cph.3g09060.jpg

24-pounder: Public Domain. National Park Service photo. http://www.nps.gov/york/historyculture/images/P10105104x6small.jpg

Gundalow: Public Domain. http://www.dover.lib.nh.us/DoverHistory/1983.htm

Persuasiveness

Witherspoon Portrait: Public Domain. https://bearspace.baylor.edu/Elmer_Duncan/www/fea_fig4b.jpg

Signing of Declaration of Independence: Public Domain. http://en.wikipedia.org/wiki/File:Declaration_independence.jpg

Resourcefulness

Oliver Wolcott Portrait: Public Domain. http://en.wikipedia.org/wiki/File:Oliver_Wolcott_Ralph_Earl.jpeg

Pouring lead for bullets: http://queencreekdailyphoto.blogspot.com/2009/11/making-bullets.html

Bullets in keg: http://smellyann.typepad.com/.a/6a00e54efa53e08833014e8bca402e970d-pi

Tearing down statue: Public Domain. http://www.connecticutsar.org/articles/king_georges_head.htm

Responsibility

Richard Henry Lee Portrait: original drawing by Linda J. Linder for *For You They Signed* by Marilyn Boyer, 2008

Richard Henry Lee standing portrait: Public Domain. http://www.history.org/almanack/people/bios/biolee.cfm

Drafting Declaration: http://ushistoryimages.com/the-declaration-of-independence.shtm

Valor

Hauling guns: Public Domain. http://www.archives.gov/research/military/american-revolution/pictures/index.html#ne

Boston from Dorchester Heights:1837, William Henry Bartlett J. T. Wilmore, Sheet: 11.2 x 17.5 cm (4 7/16 x 6 7/8 in.), Brush and sepia wash with scratched highlights on paper, Classification: Drawings, Museum of Fine Arts, Boston

Three soldiers: Public Domain. http://www.history.army.mil/html/artphoto/pripos/amsoldier3.html

Evacuation of Boston: http://fineartamerica.com/featured/lord-howe-organizes-the-british-evacuation-of-boston-in-march-1776-english-school.html

General Howe: Public Domain. http://reinsteinrevolutionper10.wikispaces.com/Battle+of+Long+Island

Wisdom

Soldiers building cabins: Public Domain. http://ushistoryimages.com/valley-forge.shtm

Washington at prayer: http://www.amazon.com/George-Washington-Prayer-Valley-10-00X9-50/dp/B003ZMRC5Q

Washington on horse: Public Domain. http://www.oneidanation.org/culture/page.aspx?id=2446

Isaac Potts House: http://freepages.history.rootsweb.ancestry.com/~wcarr1/Lossing1/Chap37.html

Endnotes

[1]The Rev. Peter Powers, *Jesus Christ the True King and Head of Government; A Sermon Preached before the General Assembly of the State of Vermont, on the Day of Their First Election, March 12, 1778 at Windsor,* Newbury-Port: Printed by John Michael, 1778, p. 18.

[2]Samuel Adams, *Writings,* Vol. IV, p. 86, "Manifesto of the Continental Congress" on October 30, 1778.

[3]John Witherspoon, *The Works of John Witherspoon,* Edinburgh: J. Ogle, 1815, Vol. IX, p. 250, "The Druid," Number III.

[4]"The American Revolution: Was it an Act of Biblical Rebellion?" article by David Barton, www.wallbuilders.com, May, 2009.

About the Authors

Marilyn Boyer is the mother of fourteen children, all home schooled from kindergarten through high school. Her passion to train up her children in the character of Christ led her to create Character Concepts Curriculum, a character curriculum for kids of all ages to equip parents in raising children of integrity!

Her many character resources, as well as books on homeschooling and Christian parenting, are available online.

About the Authors

Grace Tumas Ehrman holds a degree in history from Liberty University. Her paper, "Warlords and Samurais: Japanese Interventionists in Siberia During the Russian Civil War, 1918-1922," won an award at the 2013 Phi Alpha Theta History Conference. She specializes in American and Russian history.

ISBN 13: 978-1-68344-400-8

ISBN 13: 978-1-68344-401-5

ISBN 13: 978-1-68344-402-2

The *Legends of Faith* series brings the powerful stories of Christian heroes to life for middle and high school students! Marilyn Boyer's newest series includes engaging biographies, vibrant illustrations, and timeless truths that inspire courage and faith.

ISBN 13: 978-1-68344-403-9

VISIT MASTERBOOKS.COM — *Where Faith Grows!* — TO SEE OUR FULL LINE OF FAITH-BUILDING BOOKS OR CALL 800-999-3777

What a Character!
READERS FOR KIDS
Notable Lives from History

Inspire Students with Biographies of **Notable Lives** from **HISTORY.**

MASTERBOOKS.COM
Where Faith Grows!

America's War Heroes
Inventors and Scientists
Extraordinary Animal Heroes
Heroes of the War of Independence
Famous Women in History
Famous Pioneers and Frontiersmen
Amazing American Presidents
America's Famous Spies
Famous American Statesmen
Heroes of Early America